MAGELLAN GEOGRA~~PHIX~~

UNITED ST~~ATES~~
HISTORY ATLAS

Contents

©2000 Maps.com/MAGELLAN Geographix, 6464 Hollister Avenue, Santa Barbara, CA 93117 / 800-929-4MAP / 805-685-3100.

Visit the world's premier map website at http://www.maps.com, where you will find thousands of quality map products, driving directions, address finder, and other map- and travel-related resources. For additional educational map collections and resources, visit http://www.maps101.com.

Cover map image from a digital collection of antique maps by Visual Language Library. Author unknown, 1887.

ISBN: 1-930194-01-3

POSSIBLE MIGRATION ROUTES OF THE FIRST AMERICANS

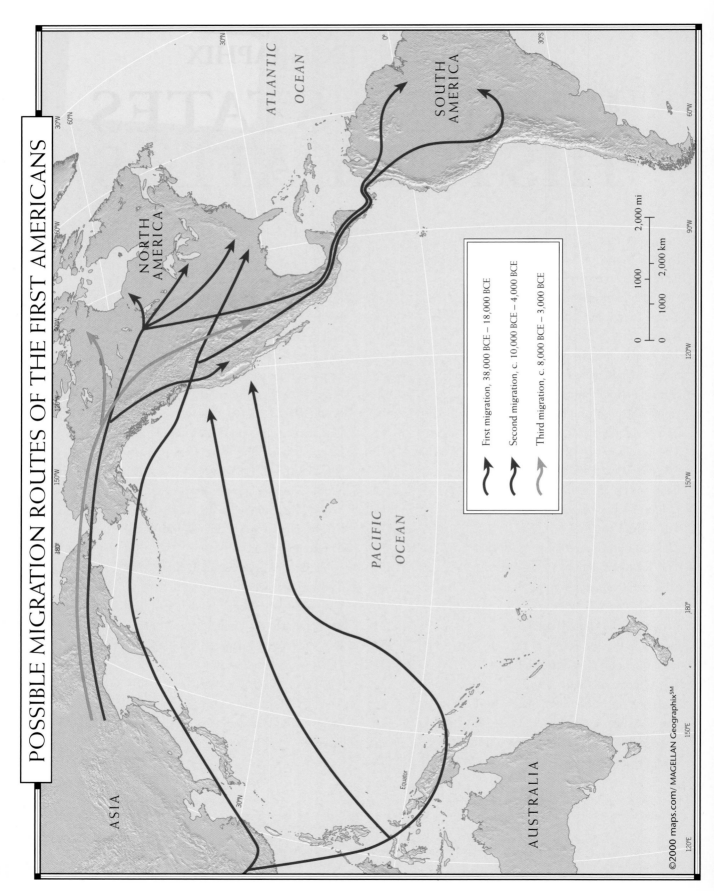

First migration, 38,000 BCE – 18,000 BCE

Second migration, c. 10,000 BCE – 4,000 BCE

Third migration, c. 8,000 BCE – 3,000 BCE

ASIA

NORTH AMERICA

SOUTH AMERICA

ATLANTIC OCEAN

PACIFIC OCEAN

AUSTRALIA

Equator

2,000 mi

2,000 km

©2000 maps.com/ MAGELLAN Geographix℠

EARLY VOYAGES OF EXPLORATION

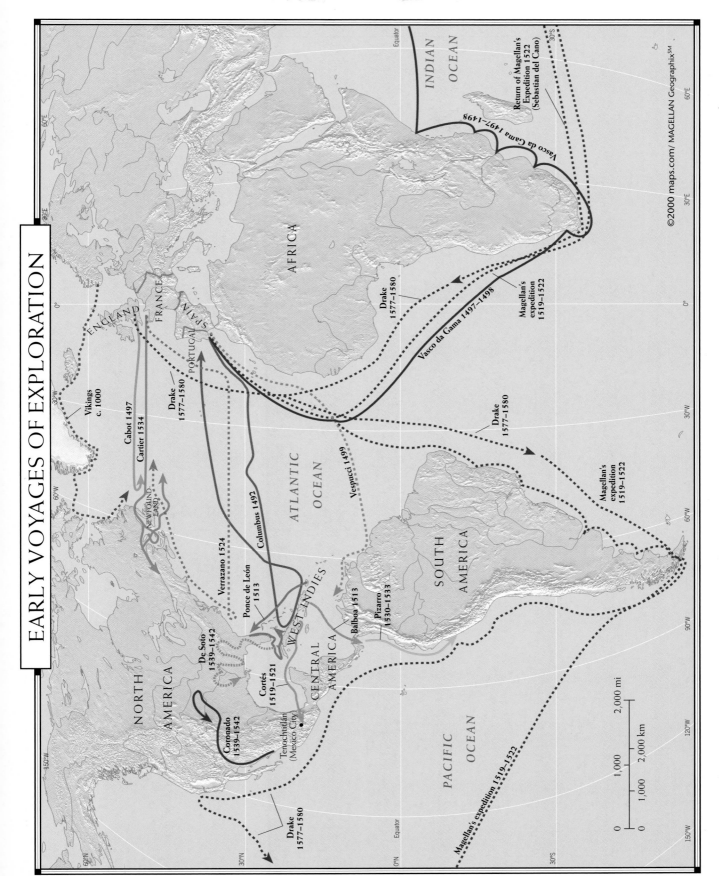

INDIAN OCEAN

Return of Magellan's Expedition 1522 (Sebastian del Cano)

Vasco da Gama 1497–1498

AFRICA

Magellan's expedition 1519–1522

Drake 1577–1580

Vasco da Gama 1497–1498

ENGLAND

FRANCE

SPAIN

PORTUGAL

Vikings c. 1000

Cabot 1497

Cartier 1534

Drake 1577–1580

Drake 1577–1580

Verrazano 1524

NEWFOUND-LAND

Columbus 1492

ATLANTIC OCEAN

Vespucci 1499

Ponce de León 1513

WEST INDIES

Balboa 1513

Pizarro 1530–1533

SOUTH AMERICA

Magellan's expedition 1519–1522

De Soto 1539–1542

Cortés 1519–1521

CENTRAL AMERICA

NORTH AMERICA

Coronado 1539–1542

Tenochtitlán (Mexico City)

PACIFIC OCEAN

Magellan's expedition 1519–1522

Drake 1577–1580

2,000 mi

2,000 km

1,000

1,000

0

0

Equator

©2000 maps.com/ MAGELLAN Geographix℠

— 3 —

EUROPEAN EXPLORATION OF NORTH AMERICA

PACIFIC

OCEAN

NORTH

AMERICA

ATLANTIC

OCEAN

Arctic Circle

Vikings, c. 1000

Henry Hudson, 1610

Vikings, c. 1000

Cartier, 1535–1536

John Cabot, 1497

Champlain, 1603–1616

Lake Superior

Lake Huron

Lake Michigan

Lake Ontario

Lake Erie

Marquette and Joliet, 1673

Hudson, 1609

La Salle, 1682

• St. Louis

De Soto, 1539–1541

• Charles Town

Mississippi R.

De Soto dies, May 21, 1542

• New Orleans

Verrazzano, 1523

Rio Grande

Coronado, 1540–1542

Ponce de León, 1513

Gulf of Mexico

Havana •

Tropic of Cancer

Drake, 1577–1580

Cortes, 1519

Caribbean Sea

Balboa, 1513

SOUTH AMERICA

60°N

45°N

30°N

15°N

120°W 90°W 60°W 30°W

→	Vikings
→	Dutch
→	English
→	French
→	Spanish

0   500   1,000 mi

0   500   1,000 km

©2000 maps.com/ MAGELLAN Geographix℠

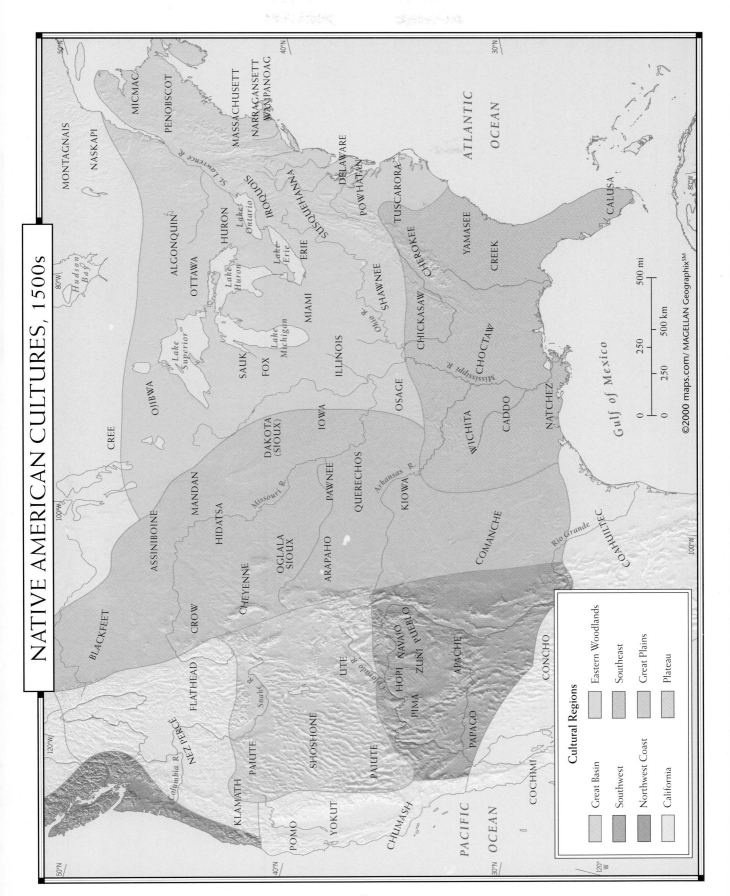

NATIVE AMERICAN CULTURES, 1500s

ATLANTIC OCEAN

PACIFIC OCEAN

Gulf of Mexico

Hudson Bay

MONTAGNAIS
NASKAPI
MICMAC
PENOBSCOT
MASSACHUSETT
NARRAGANSETT
WAMPANOAG
DELAWARE
POWHATAN
TUSCARORA
YAMASEE
CALUSA
CREEK
CHEROKEE
CHICKASAW
CHOCTAW
NATCHEZ
CADDO
WICHITA
CREE
OJIBWA
ALGONQUIN
OTTAWA
HURON
IROQUOIS
SIOUX
SUSQUEHANNA
ERIE
SHAWNEE
MIAMI
ILLINOIS
SAUK
FOX
OSAGE
DAKOTA (SIOUX)
IOWA
PAWNEE
QUERECHOS
KIOWA
ASSINIBOINE
MANDAN
HIDATSA
OGLALA SIOUX
ARAPAHO
COMANCHE
COAHUILTEC
CONCHO
BLACKFEET
CROW
CHEYENNE
FLATHEAD
NEZ PERCÉ
PAIUTE
SHOSHONE
UTE
PAIUTE
NAVAJO
HOPI
ZUÑI PUEBLO
PIMA
APACHE
PAPAGO
KLAMATH
POMO
YOKUT
CHUMASH
COCHIMI

St. Lawrence R.
Lake Ontario
Lake Erie
Lake Huron
Lake Superior
Lake Michigan
Ohio R.
Mississippi R.
Arkansas R.
Missouri R.
Rio Grande
Columbia R.
Snake R.
Colorado R.

©2000 maps.com/ MAGELLAN Geographix℠

500 mi
500 km
250
250
0
0

Cultural Regions

Great Basin		Eastern Woodlands
Southwest		Southeast
Northwest Coast		Great Plains
California		Plateau

50°N 40°N 30°N
50°W 40°N 30°N 80°W
80°W 100°W 100°W 120°W 120°W

— 5 —

NATIVE AMERICAN NATIONS, c. 1750

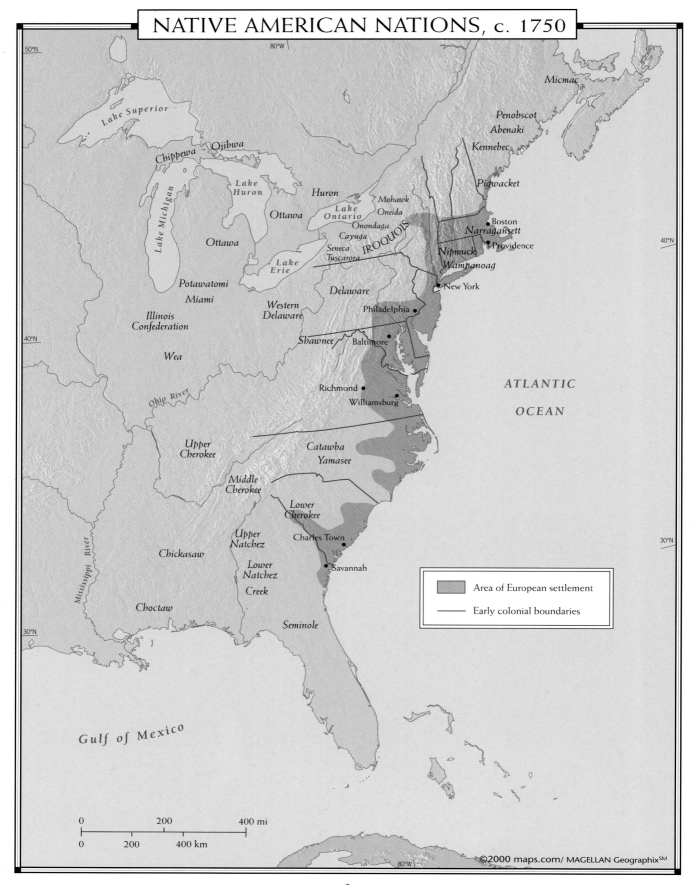

Micmac

Penobscot
Abenaki
Kennebec

Pigwacket

Lake Superior

Ojibwa

Chippewa

Boston •
Narragansett
• Providence

**Lake
Huron**

Huron

Ottawa

**Lake
Ontario**

Mohawk
Oneida
Onondaga
Cayuga
Seneca
Tuscarora

IROQUOIS

Nipmuck
Wampanoag

Lake Michigan

Ottawa

**Lake
Erie**

Potawatomi
Miami

*Illinois
Confederation*

Delaware

New York •

*Western
Delaware*

Philadelphia •

Wea

Shawnee

Baltimore •

Ohio River

Richmond •

Williamsburg •

ATLANTIC

OCEAN

*Upper
Cherokee*

Catawba
Yamasee

*Middle
Cherokee*

*Lower
Cherokee*

Charles Town •

*Upper
Natchez*

Chickasaw

*Lower
Natchez*

Creek

Savannah •

Mississippi River

Choctaw

Seminole

	Area of European settlement
	Early colonial boundaries

Gulf of Mexico

0	200	400 mi
0	200	400 km

©2000 maps.com/ MAGELLAN Geographix℠

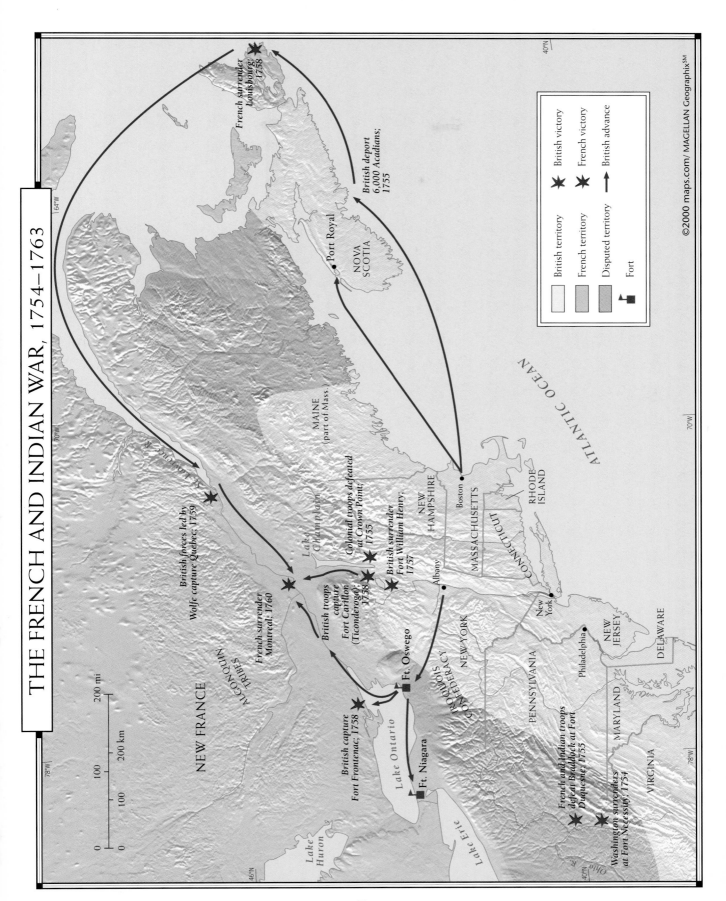

THE FRENCH AND INDIAN WAR, 1754–1763

©2000 maps.com/ MAGELLAN Geographix℠

Legend:
- British victory
- French victory
- British advance
- British territory
- French territory
- Disputed territory
- Fort

French surrender Louisbourg; 1758

British deport 6,000 Acadians; 1755

Port Royal

NOVA SCOTIA

ATLANTIC OCEAN

MAINE (part of Mass.)

NEW HAMPSHIRE

Boston

MASSACHUSETTS

RHODE ISLAND

CONNECTICUT

Albany

New York

NEW YORK

IROQUOIS CONFEDERACY

NEW JERSEY

DELAWARE

Philadelphia

PENNSYLVANIA

MARYLAND

VIRGINIA

British forces led by Wolfe capture Quebec; 1759

French surrender Montreal; 1760

Colonial troops defeated at Crown Point; 1755

British surrender Fort William Henry; 1757

British troops capture Fort Carillon (Ticonderoga); 1758

Lake Champlain

NEW FRANCE

ALGONQUIN TRIBES

St. Lawrence R.

British capture Fort Frontenac; 1758

Ft. Oswego

Lake Ontario

Ft. Niagara

Lake Erie

Lake Huron

Ohio R.

French and Indian troops defeat Braddock at Fort Duquesne; 1755

Washington surrenders at Fort Necessity; 1754

200 mi
0   100   200 km

64°W
70°W
78°W
40°N
46°N
70°W
78°W

SLAVE TRADE ROUTES, 1400s–1800s

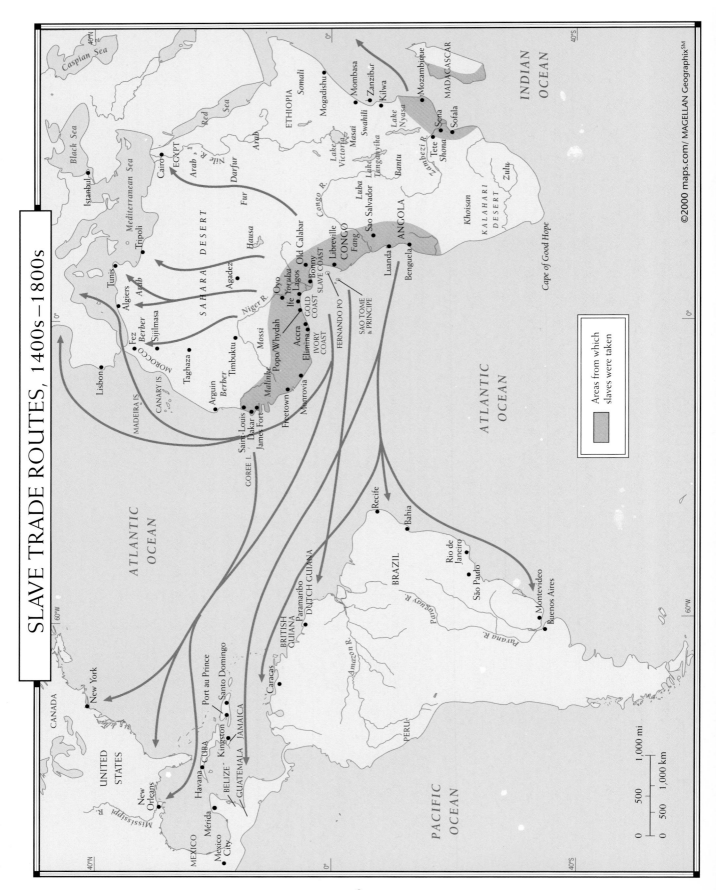

Areas from which slaves were taken

©2000 maps.com/ MAGELLAN Geographix℠

INDIAN OCEAN

ATLANTIC OCEAN

ATLANTIC OCEAN

PACIFIC OCEAN

Caspian Sea

Black Sea

Mediterranean Sea

Red Sea

ETHIOPIA
Somali
Mogadishu
Mombasa
Zanzibar
Kilwa
Mozambique
MADAGASCAR
Sena
Sofala
Lake Nyasa
Tete
Shona
Zambezi R.
Bantu
Lake Tanganyika
Luba
Lake Victoria
Masai
Swahili
Khoisan
KALAHARI DESERT
Zulu
Cape of Good Hope

Cairo
EGYPT
Nile R.
Arab
Arab
Darfur
Fur
SAHARA DESERT
Hausa
Agadez
Niger R.
Oyo
Yoruba
Ile
Lagos
Bonny
GOLD COAST
SLAVE COAST
Old Calabar
Libreville
Fang
CONGO
Congo R.
Sao Salvador
ANGOLA
Luanda
Benguela
SAO TOME & PRINCIPE
FERNANDO PO

Istanbul
Tripoli
Tunis
Algiers
Arab
Berber
Fez
Sijilmasa
MOROCCO
Berber
Taghaza
Timbuktu
Mossi
Arguin
Berber
Malinke
Saint-Louis
Dakar
James Fort
Freetown
Monrovia
Accra
Elimina
IVORY COAST
Popo/Whydah

Lisbon
MADEIRA IS.
CANARY IS.
COREE I.

New York
UNITED STATES
New Orleans
Mississippi R.
CANADA
MEXICO
Mexico City
Mérida
Havana
CUBA
BELIZE
GUATEMALA
Kingston
JAMAICA
Port au Prince
Santo Domingo
Caracas
BRITISH GUIANA
DUTCH GUIANA
Paramaribo
PERU
Amazon R.
BRAZIL
Recife
Bahia
Rio de Janeiro
São Paulo
Paraguay R.
Paraná R.
Montevideo
Buenos Aires

1,000 mi
1,000 km
500
500
500
0
0

– 8 –

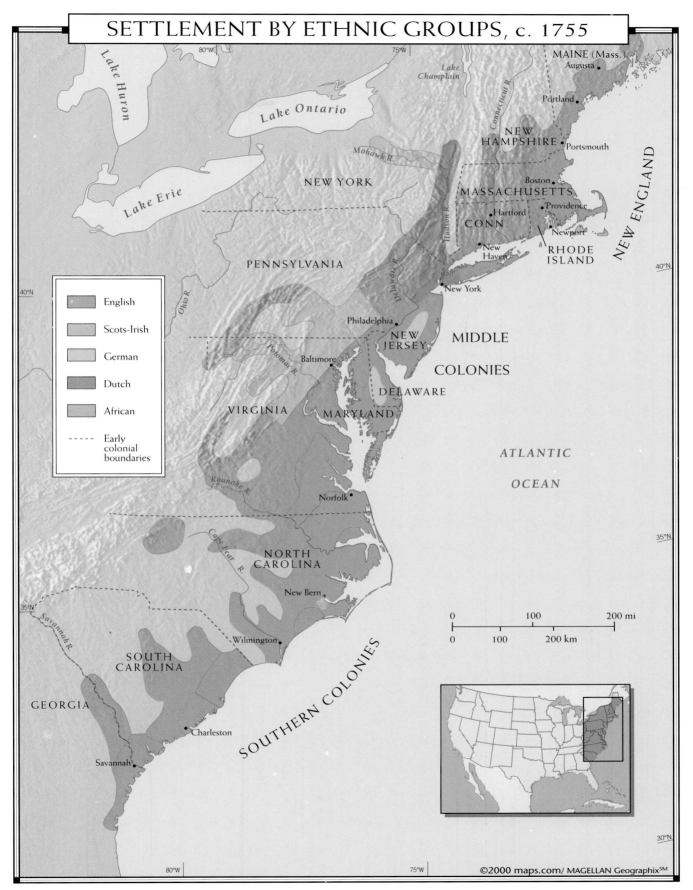

SETTLEMENT BY ETHNIC GROUPS, c. 1755

Legend:
- English
- Scots-Irish
- German
- Dutch
- African
- Early colonial boundaries

Lake Huron
Lake Erie
Lake Ontario
Lake Champlain

MAINE (Mass.)
Augusta
Portland
NEW HAMPSHIRE
Portsmouth
Boston
MASSACHUSETTS
Providence
Hartford
CONN.
Newport
New Haven
RHODE ISLAND
NEW ENGLAND

NEW YORK
Mohawk R.
Hudson R.
Connecticut R.

PENNSYLVANIA
Delaware R.
New York

Philadelphia
NEW JERSEY
MIDDLE COLONIES

Ohio R.
Potomac R.
Baltimore
DELAWARE
VIRGINIA
MARYLAND

ATLANTIC OCEAN

Roanoke R.
Norfolk

Cape Fear R.
NORTH CAROLINA
New Bern

Wilmington

SOUTH CAROLINA
Savannah R.
GEORGIA
Charleston
Savannah

SOUTHERN COLONIES

80°W   75°W
40°N
35°N
30°N

0   100   200 mi
0   100   200 km

©2000 maps.com/ MAGELLAN Geographix℠

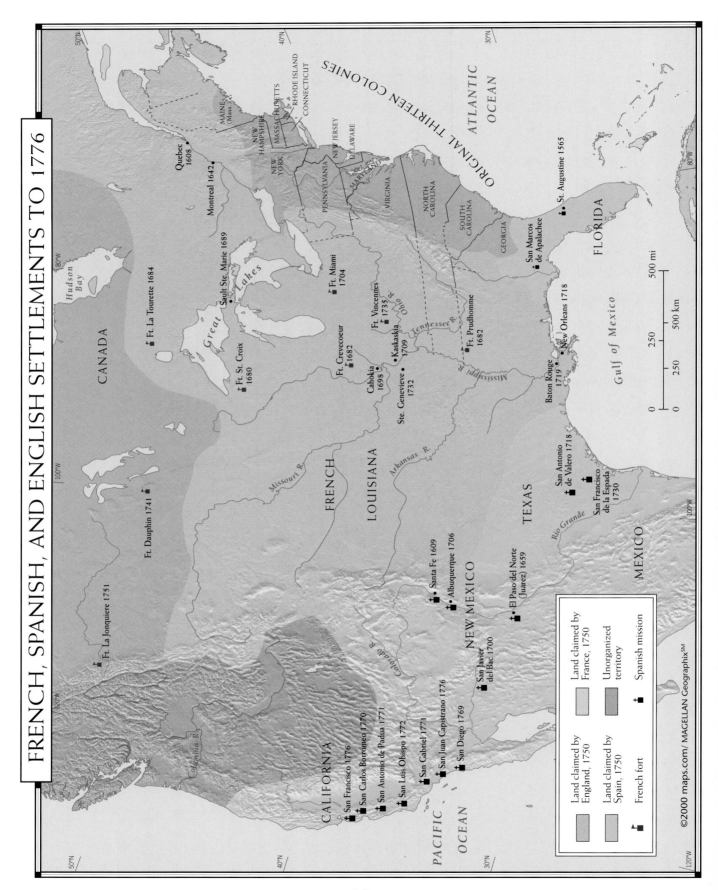

FRENCH, SPANISH, AND ENGLISH SETTLEMENTS TO 1776

Hudson Bay

CANADA

Great Lakes

Ft. La Tourette 1684

Ft. Dauphin 1741

Sault Ste. Marie 1689

Ft. St. Croix 1680

Quebec 1608

Montreal 1642

MAINE (Mass.)

NEW HAMPSHIRE

MASSACHUSETTS

RHODE ISLAND

CONNECTICUT

NEW YORK

NEW JERSEY

PENNSYLVANIA

DELAWARE

MARYLAND

VIRGINIA

NORTH CAROLINA

SOUTH CAROLINA

GEORGIA

ORIGINAL THIRTEEN COLONIES

ATLANTIC OCEAN

Ft. Miami 1704

Ft. Crevecoeur 1682

Ft. Vincennes 1735

Kaskaskia 1709

Cahokia 1698

Ohio R.

Tennessee R.

Ft. Prudhomme 1682

Mississippi R.

Ste. Genevieve 1732

Missouri R.

FRENCH LOUISIANA

Arkansas R.

San Marcos de Apalachee

St. Augustine 1565

FLORIDA

New Orleans 1718

Baton Rouge 1719

Gulf of Mexico

Ft. La Jonquiere 1751

Columbia R.

CALIFORNIA

San Francisco 1776

San Carlos Borromeo 1770

San Antonio de Padua 1771

San Luis Obispo 1772

San Gabriel 1771

San Juan Capistrano 1776

San Diego 1769

San Javier del Bac 1700

NEW MEXICO

Santa Fe 1609

Albuquerque 1706

El Paso del Norte (Juarez) 1659

TEXAS

San Antonio de Valero 1718

San Francisco de la Espada 1730

Rio Grande

MEXICO

PACIFIC OCEAN

500 mi

500 km

250

250

0

0

©2000 maps.com/ MAGELLAN Geographix℠

Land claimed by England, 1750

Land claimed by Spain, 1750

French fort

Land claimed by France, 1750

Unorganized territory

Spanish mission

50°N

40°N

30°N

120°W

110°W

100°W

80°W

80°W

50°W

40°W

— 10 —

THE REVOLUTIONARY WAR IN THE NORTH AND WEST, 1776–1780

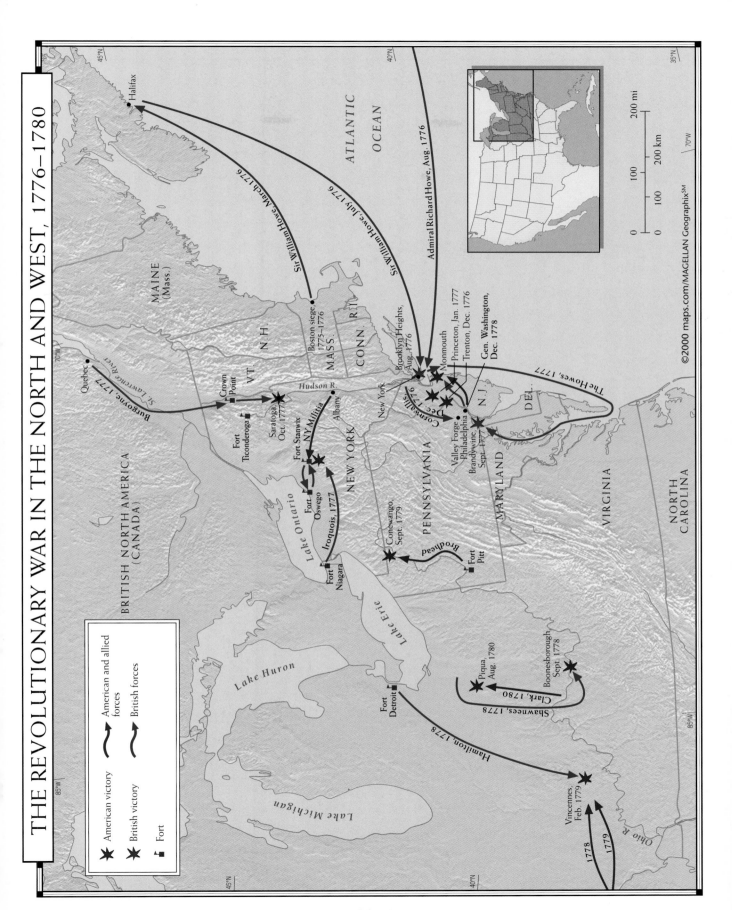

Legend:
- American and allied forces
- British forces
- American victory
- British victory
- Fort

©2000 maps.com/MAGELLAN Geographix[SM]

Halifax

ATLANTIC OCEAN

Sir William Howe, March 1776

Sir William Howe, July 1776

Admiral Richard Howe, Aug. 1776

MAINE (Mass.)

Boston siege 1775–1776

N.H.

MASS.

CONN.

R.I.

Quebec

St. Lawrence River

Burgoyne, 1777

Crown Point

VT.

Fort Ticonderoga

Saratoga, Oct. 1777

Hudson R.

Fort Stanwix

NY Militia

Albany

New York

Brooklyn Heights, Aug. 1776

Monmouth

Princeton, Jan. 1777

Trenton, Dec. 1776

Gen. Washington, Dec. 1778

Cornwallis, Dec. 1776

N.J.

Valley Forge

Philadelphia

Brandywine, Sept. 1777

DEL.

The Howes, 1777

BRITISH NORTH AMERICA (CANADA)

Fort Oswego

Iroquois, 1777

NEW YORK

Conewango, Sept. 1779

Brodhead

Fort Pitt

PENNSYLVANIA

MARYLAND

VIRGINIA

NORTH CAROLINA

Fort Niagara

Lake Ontario

Lake Erie

Lake Huron

Lake Michigan

Fort Detroit

Hamilton, 1778

Piqua, Aug. 1780

Clark, 1780

Shawnees, 1778

Boonesborough, Sept. 1778

Vincennes, Feb. 1779

Ohio R.

1778

1779

200 mi

200 km

0   100   200

0   100   200

45°N

40°N

35°N

85°W

70°W

85°W

70°W

45°N

40°N

THE REVOLUTIONARY WAR IN THE SOUTH, 1778–1781

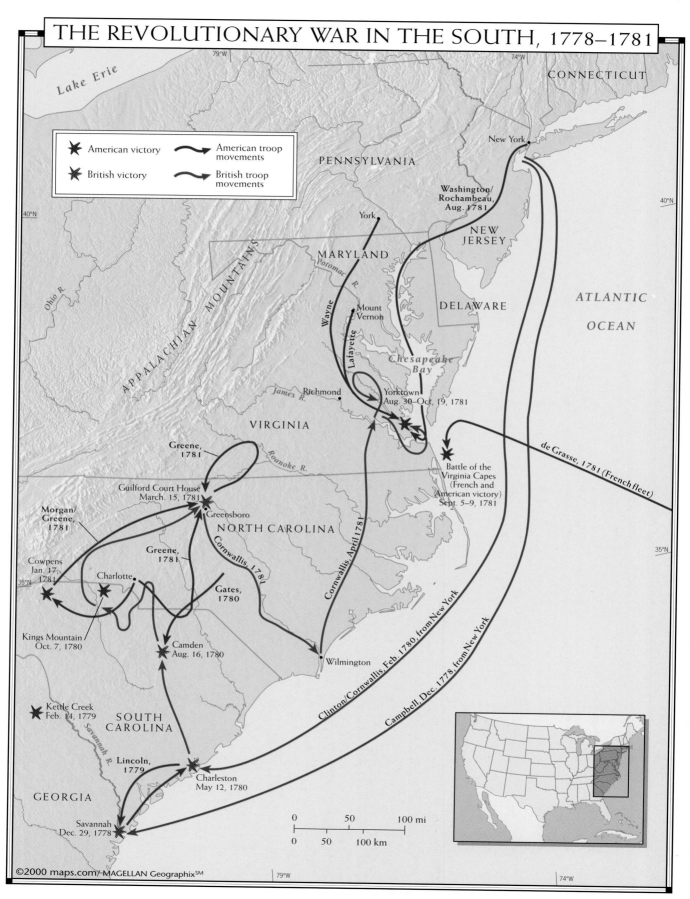

Legend:
- ✦ American victory
- ✦ British victory
- American troop movements
- British troop movements

Lake Erie

CONNECTICUT

PENNSYLVANIA

New York

Washington/ Rochambeau, Aug. 1781

NEW JERSEY

MARYLAND

York

Potomac R.

DELAWARE

ATLANTIC OCEAN

Wayne

Mount Vernon

Lafayette

Chesapeake Bay

APPALACHIAN MOUNTAINS

Ohio R.

James R.

Richmond

Yorktown
Aug. 30–Oct. 19, 1781

VIRGINIA

Roanoke R.

Greene, 1781

de Grasse, 1781 (French fleet)

Battle of the Virginia Capes (French and American victory) Sept. 5–9, 1781

Guilford Court House
March. 15, 1781

Greensboro

Morgan/ Greene, 1781

Greene, 1781

NORTH CAROLINA

Cornwallis, 1781

Cowpens
Jan. 17, 1781

Charlotte

Gates, 1780

Cornwallis, April 1781

Kings Mountain
Oct. 7, 1780

Camden
Aug. 16, 1780

Wilmington

Clinton/Cornwallis, Feb. 1780, from New York

Kettle Creek
Feb. 14, 1779

SOUTH CAROLINA

Campbell, Dec. 1778, from New York

Savannah R.

Lincoln, 1779

Charleston
May 12, 1780

GEORGIA

Savannah
Dec. 29, 1778

| 0 | 50 | 100 mi |
| 0 | 50 | 100 km |

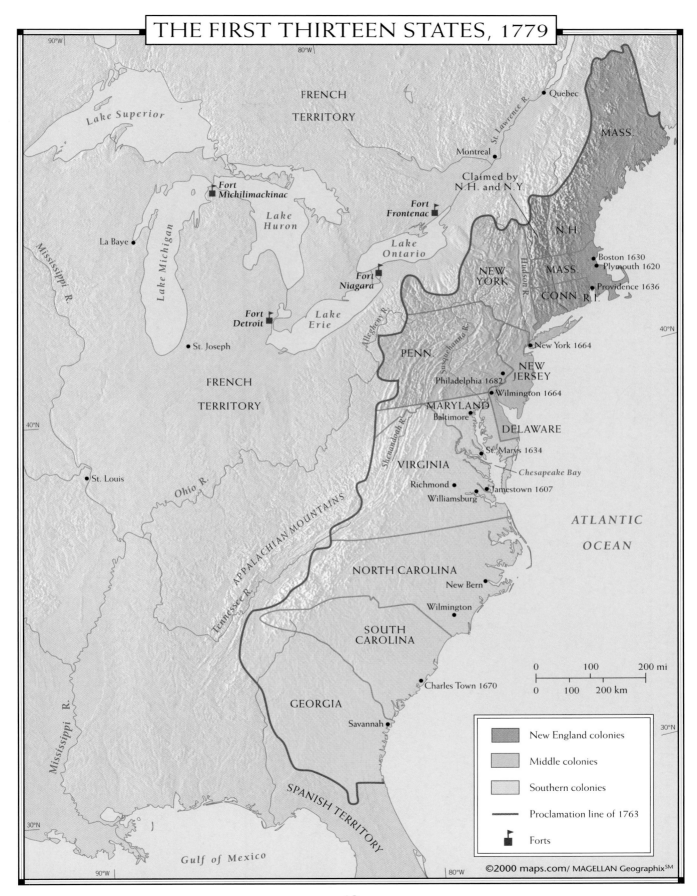

THE FIRST THIRTEEN STATES, 1779

90°W

80°W

FRENCH TERRITORY

• Quebec

St. Lawrence R.

MASS.

Montreal •

Claimed by N.H. and N.Y.

Lake Superior

Fort Michilimackinac

Lake Huron

Fort Frontenac

N.H.

La Baye •

Lake Michigan

Lake Ontario

Fort Niagara

Boston 1630
Plymouth 1620

NEW YORK

MASS.

Hudson R.

CONN. R.I.

Providence 1636

40°N

Fort Detroit

Lake Erie

Allegheny R.

New York 1664

• St. Joseph

Susquehanna R.

PENN.

NEW JERSEY

FRENCH TERRITORY

Philadelphia 1682

Wilmington 1664

MARYLAND

DELAWARE

Shenandoah R.

Baltimore •

• St. Louis

Ohio R.

St. Marys 1634

VIRGINIA

Chesapeake Bay

Richmond •

Jamestown 1607

Williamsburg •

ATLANTIC OCEAN

APPALACHIAN MOUNTAINS

Tennessee R.

NORTH CAROLINA

New Bern •

Wilmington •

SOUTH CAROLINA

Mississippi R.

0   100   200 mi

0   100   200 km

Charles Town 1670

GEORGIA

30°N

Savannah •

SPANISH TERRITORY

	New England colonies
	Middle colonies
	Southern colonies
—	Proclamation line of 1763
▪	Forts

Mississippi R.

30°N

Gulf of Mexico

90°W

80°W

©2000 maps.com/ MAGELLAN Geographix℠

40°N

30°N

LOUISIANA PURCHASE AND WESTERN EXPLORATION, 1804–1807

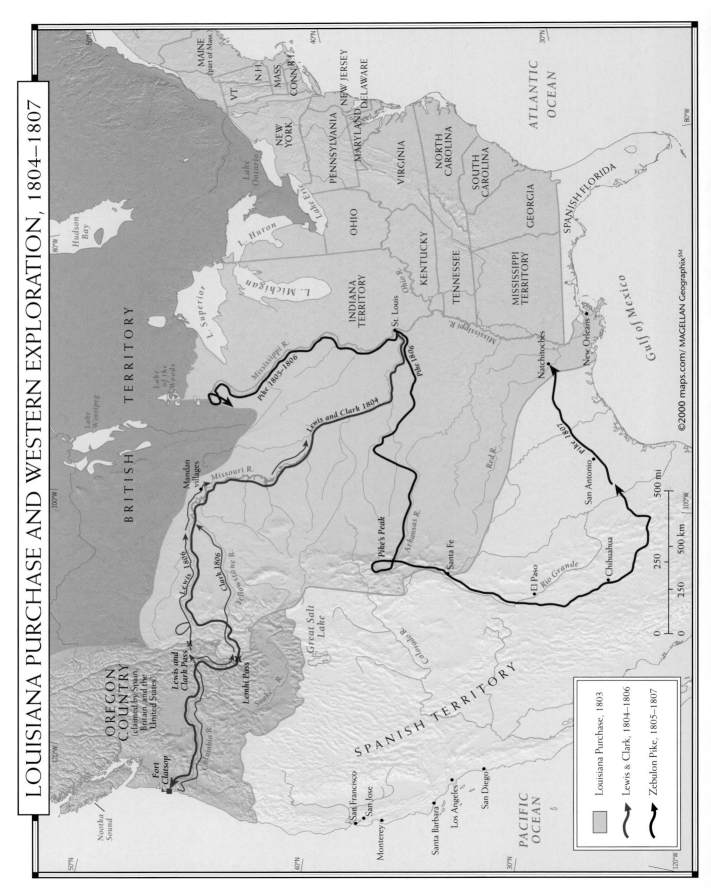

©2000 maps.com/ MAGELLAN Geographix℠

MAINE
(part of Mass.)

VT. N.H. MASS CONN. R.I.

NEW YORK

NEW JERSEY

PENNSYLVANIA

MARYLAND DELAWARE

VIRGINIA

NORTH CAROLINA

SOUTH CAROLINA

GEORGIA

SPANISH FLORIDA

ATLANTIC OCEAN

OHIO

KENTUCKY

TENNESSEE

MISSISSIPPI TERRITORY

INDIANA TERRITORY

St. Louis

Ohio R.

Mississippi R.

Gulf of Mexico

New Orleans

Natchitoches

BRITISH TERRITORY

Hudson Bay

Lake Winnipeg

L. Superior

L. Michigan

L. Huron

Lake Ontario

Lake Erie

Lake of the Woods

Mississippi R.

Pike 1805–1806

Lewis and Clark 1804

Pike 1806

Mandan villages

Missouri R.

Pike 1807

Red R.

Arkansas R.

San Antonio

Santa Fe

Pike's Peak

Chihuahua

El Paso

Rio Grande

Lewis 1806

Clark 1806

Yellowstone R.

Lemhi Pass

Lewis and Clark Pass

Great Salt Lake

Snake R.

Colorado R.

OREGON COUNTRY
(claimed by Spain, Britain, and the United States)

Columbia R.

Fort Clatsop

Nootka Sound

PACIFIC OCEAN

San Francisco

San Jose

Monterey

Santa Barbara

Los Angeles

San Diego

SPANISH TERRITORY

500 mi

500 km

250

250

0

0

Louisiana Purchase, 1803	
Lewis & Clark, 1804–1806	
Zebulon Pike, 1805–1807	

CALIFORNIA'S EARLY SETTLEMENTS, 1769–1823

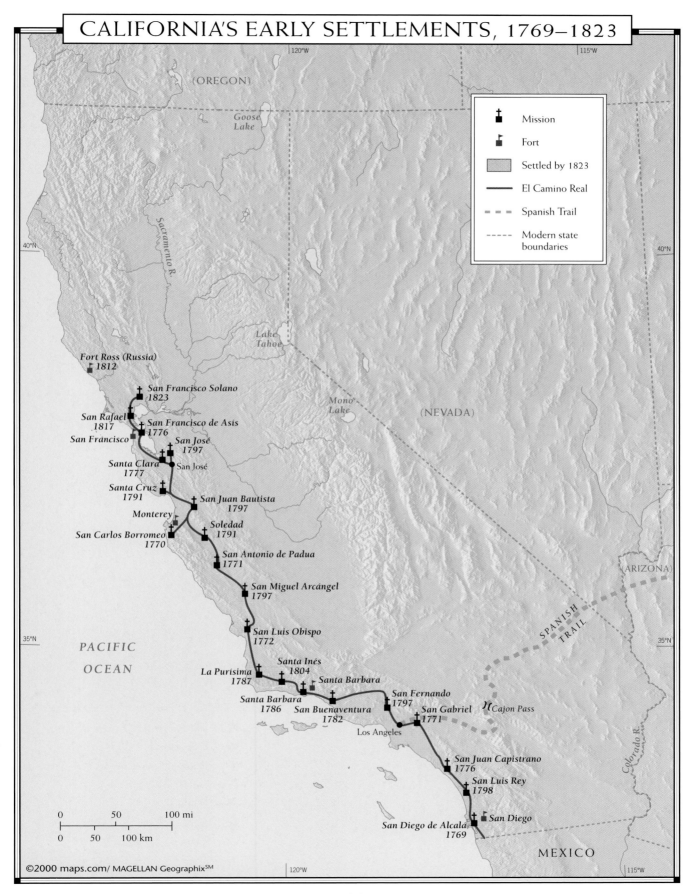

(OREGON)

Goose
Lake

120°W   115°W

	Mission
⚑	Fort
	Settled by 1823
—	El Camino Real
- - -	Spanish Trail
- - -	Modern state boundaries

40°N

Sacramento R.

Lake
Tahoe

Fort Ross (Russia)
1812

San Francisco Solano
1823

San Rafael
1817
San Francisco de Asis
1776
San Francisco

San José
1797

Santa Clara
1777   San José

Santa Cruz
1791

San Juan Bautista
1797

Monterey

Soledad
1791
San Carlos Borromeo
1770

San Antonio de Padua
1771

San Miguel Arcángel
1797

San Luis Obispo
1772

Santa Inés
1804
La Purisima
1787   Santa Barbara

Santa Barbara   San Fernando
1786   1797
San Buenaventura   San Gabriel
1782   1771
              Los Angeles

Mono
Lake

(NEVADA)

(ARIZONA)

SPANISH
TRAIL

Cajon Pass

40°N

35°N

PACIFIC
OCEAN

San Juan Capistrano
1776

San Luis Rey
1798

San Diego
San Diego de Alcalá
1769

35°N

Colorado R.

0	50	100 mi
0	50	100 km

MEXICO

120°W   115°W

©2000 maps.com/ MAGELLAN Geographix℠

THE WAR OF 1812

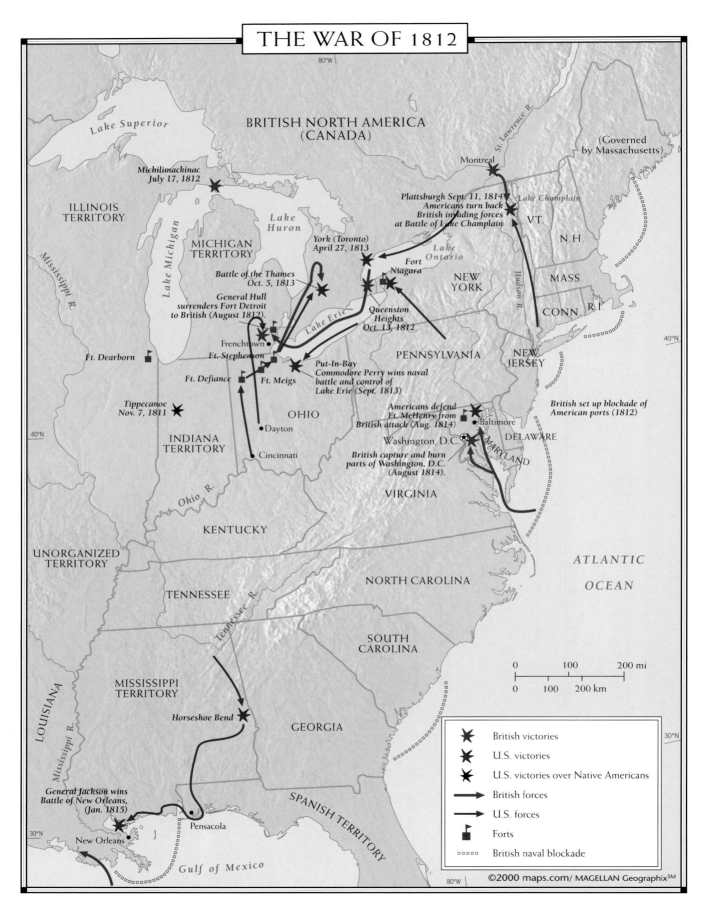

BRITISH NORTH AMERICA
(CANADA)

Lake Superior

*Michilimackinac
July 17, 1812*

ILLINOIS
TERRITORY

Lake
Huron

MICHIGAN
TERRITORY

*York (Toronto)
April 27, 1813*

Lake
Ontario

Montreal

St. Lawrence R.

(Governed
by Massachusetts)

*Plattsburgh Sept. 11, 1814
Americans turn back
British invading forces
at Battle of Lake Champlain*

Lake Champlain

VT.

N.H.

*Battle of the Thames
Oct. 5, 1813*

*General Hull
surrenders Fort Detroit
to British (August 1812).*

Lake Erie

Fort
Niagara

NEW
YORK

MASS.

Hudson R.

CONN.   R.I.

Ft. Dearborn

Frenchtown

Ft. Stephenson

Ft. Defiance   Ft. Meigs

*Queenston
Heights
Oct. 13, 1812*

PENNSYLVANIA

NEW
JERSEY

40°N

*Tippecanoe
Nov. 7, 1811*

OHIO

• Dayton

INDIANA
TERRITORY

• Cincinnati

*Put-In-Bay
Commodore Perry wins naval
battle and control of
Lake Erie (Sept. 1813)*

*Americans defend
Ft. McHenry from
British attack (Aug. 1814)*

• Baltimore

Washington, D.C. ✪

*British set up blockade of
American ports (1812)*

DELAWARE

MARYLAND

*British capture and burn
parts of Washington, D.C.
(August 1814).*

VIRGINIA

KENTUCKY

Ohio R.

ATLANTIC

OCEAN

UNORGANIZED
TERRITORY

NORTH CAROLINA

TENNESSEE

Tennessee R.

SOUTH
CAROLINA

0   100   200 mi

0   100   200 km

MISSISSIPPI
TERRITORY

Horseshoe Bend

GEORGIA

LOUISIANA

Mississippi R.

*General Jackson wins
Battle of New Orleans,
(Jan. 1815)*

SPANISH TERRITORY

30°N

• Pensacola

New Orleans •

Gulf of Mexico

✶	British victories
✴	U.S. victories
✷	U.S. victories over Native Americans
→	British forces
→	U.S. forces
■	Forts
▫▫▫	British naval blockade

©2000 maps.com/ MAGELLAN Geographix℠

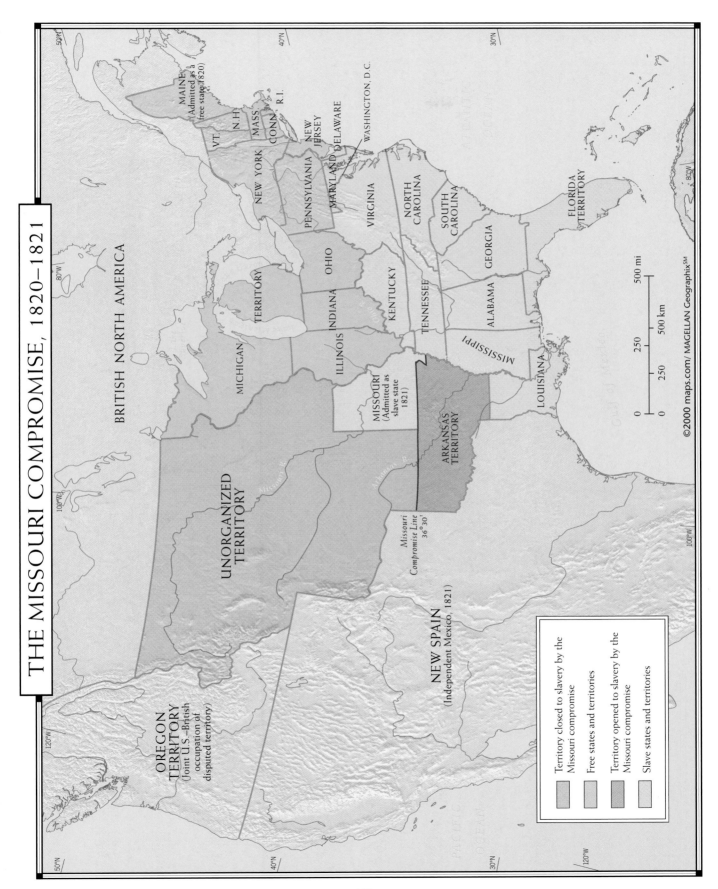

THE MISSOURI COMPROMISE, 1820–1821

BRITISH NORTH AMERICA

MAINE (Admitted as a free state 1820)

VT.

N. H.

MASS.

CONN. R.I.

NEW YORK

NEW JERSEY

PENNSYLVANIA

MARYLAND DELAWARE

WASHINGTON, D.C.

VIRGINIA

NORTH CAROLINA

SOUTH CAROLINA

GEORGIA

ALABAMA

FLORIDA TERRITORY

ATLANTIC OCEAN

MICHIGAN TERRITORY

OHIO

INDIANA

ILLINOIS

KENTUCKY

TENNESSEE

MISSISSIPPI

MISSOURI (Admitted as a slave state 1821)

LOUISIANA

ARKANSAS TERRITORY

Missouri Compromise Line 36°30'

UNORGANIZED TERRITORY

NEW SPAIN (Independent Mexico, 1821)

OREGON TERRITORY (Joint U.S.–British occupation of disputed territory)

Gulf of Mexico

PACIFIC OCEAN

Missouri R.

Arkansas R.

©2000 maps.com / MAGELLAN Geographix℠

500 mi

500 km

250

250

250

0

0

Territory closed to slavery by the Missouri compromise

Free states and territories

Territory opened to slavery by the Missouri compromise

Slave states and territories

50°N

40°N

30°N

120°W

100°W

80°W

120°W

100°W

80°W

40°N

30°N

50°N

40°N

30°N

THE TEXAS REVOLUTION, 1835–1836

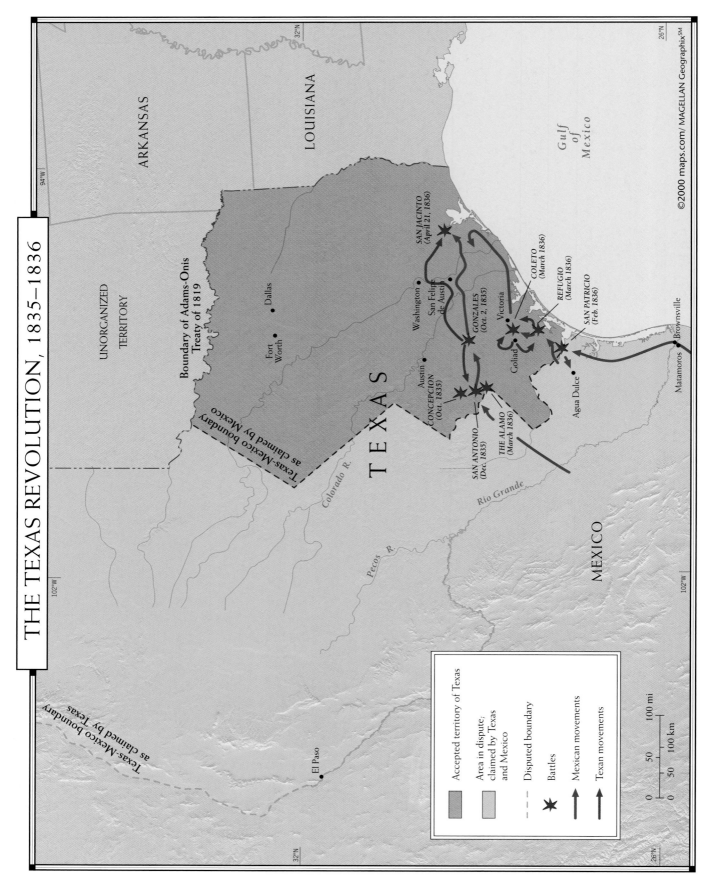

ARKANSAS

LOUISIANA

UNORGANIZED
TERRITORY

Boundary of Adams-Onis
Treaty of 1819

Dallas

Fort
Worth

Texas-Mexico boundary
as claimed by Mexico

T E X A S

Austin

CONCEPCION
(Oct. 1835)

SAN ANTONIO
(Dec. 1835)

THE ALAMO
(March 1836)

Washington

San Felipe
de Austin

GONZALES
(Oct. 2, 1835)

Victoria

Coliad

Agua Dulce

SAN JACINTO
(April 21, 1836)

COLETO
(March 1836)

REFUGIO
(March 1836)

SAN PATRICIO
(Feb. 1836)

*Gulf
of
Mexico*

Colorado R.

Pecos R.

Rio Grande

MEXICO

El Paso

Brownsville

Matamoros

Texas-Mexico boundary
as claimed by Texas

©2000 maps.com/ MAGELLAN Geographix℠

Legend

- Accepted territory of Texas
- Area in dispute; claimed by Texas and Mexico
- Disputed boundary
- Battles
- Mexican movements
- Texan movements

0   50   100 mi
0   50   100 km

32°N   94°W   102°W   26°N

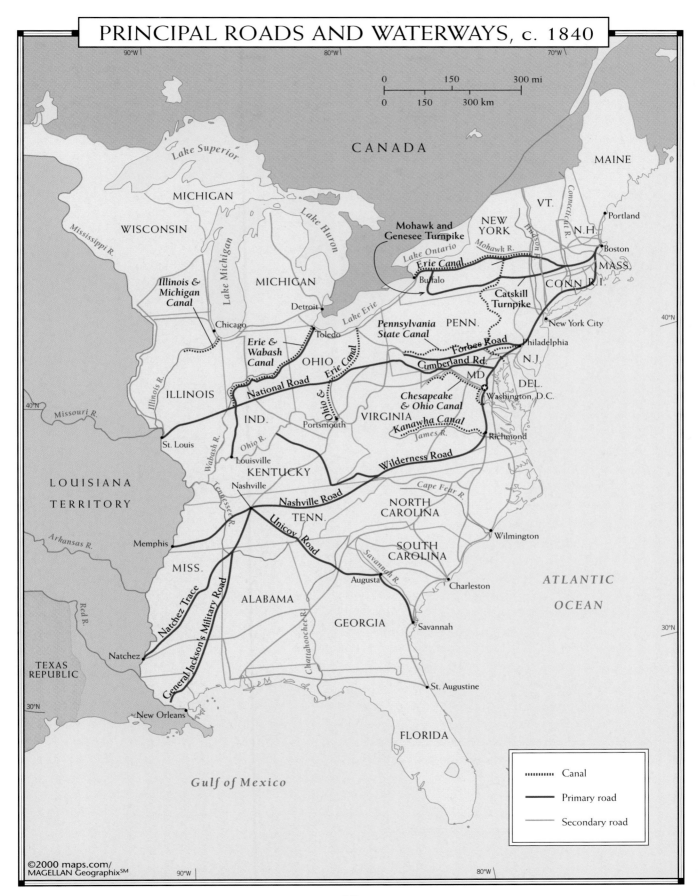

PRINCIPAL ROADS AND WATERWAYS, c. 1840

CANADA

MAINE

Lake Superior

MICHIGAN

WISCONSIN

Mississippi R.

VT.

N.H.

NEW YORK

Lake Ontario

Mohawk and Genesee Turnpike

Portland

Boston

MASS.

CONN. R.I.

Erie Canal

Mohawk R.

Hudson R.

Connecticut R.

Lake Huron

Lake Michigan

MICHIGAN

Illinois & Michigan Canal

Detroit

Lake Erie

Buffalo

Catskill Turnpike

New York City

PENN.

Pennsylvania State Canal

Forbes Road

Philadelphia

N.J.

Chicago

Toledo

Erie & Wabash Canal

OHIO

Ohio & Erie Canal

National Road

Cumberland Rd.

MD

Washington, D.C.

DEL.

ILLINOIS

Illinois R.

IND.

Ohio & Erie Canal

Portsmouth

VIRGINIA

Chesapeake & Ohio Canal

Kanawha Canal

James R.

Richmond

St. Louis

Wabash R.

Ohio R.

Louisville

KENTUCKY

Nashville

Wilderness Road

Missouri R.

40°N

LOUISIANA TERRITORY

Arkansas R.

Tennessee R.

Nashville Road

TENN.

NORTH CAROLINA

Cape Fear R.

Memphis

Unicoy Road

Savannah R.

SOUTH CAROLINA

Wilmington

MISS.

Natchez Trace

ALABAMA

Augusta

Charleston

ATLANTIC OCEAN

Chattahoochee R.

GEORGIA

Savannah

General Jackson's Military Road

TEXAS REPUBLIC

Red R.

Natchez

St. Augustine

30°N

New Orleans

FLORIDA

Gulf of Mexico

90°W   80°W   70°W

0   150   300 mi
0   150   300 km

40°N

30°N

©2000 maps.com/
MAGELLAN Geographix℠

90°W   80°W

....	Canal
——	Primary road
——	Secondary road

— 19 —

THE MEXICAN WAR, 1846–1848

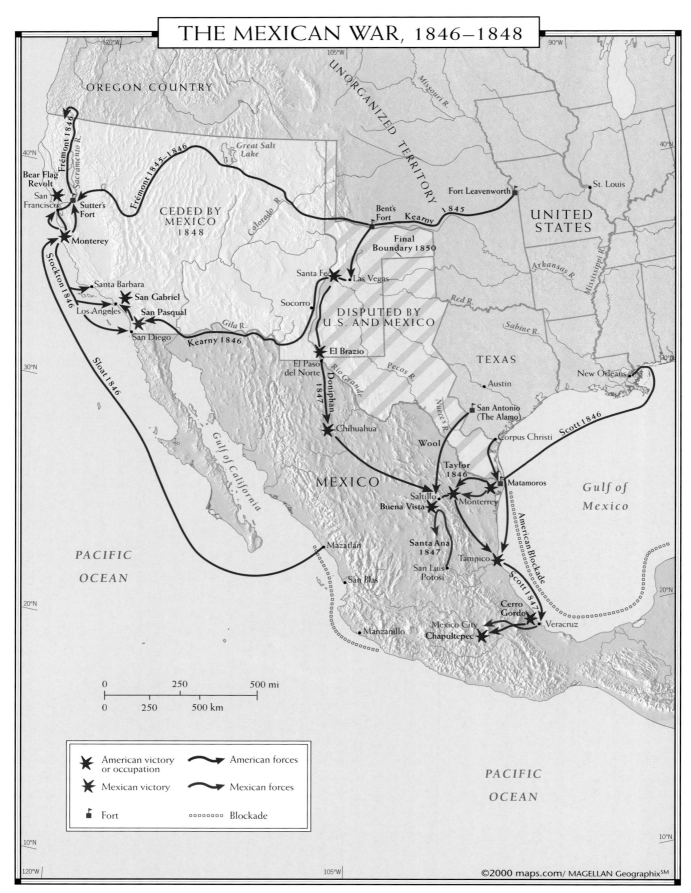

OREGON COUNTRY

UNORGANIZED TERRITORY

UNITED STATES

St. Louis

Missouri R.

Fort Leavenworth

Kearny 1845

Bent's Fort

Frémont 1846

Bear Flag Revolt

San Francisco

Sutter's Fort

Sacramento R.

Frémont 1845–1846

Great Salt Lake

CEDED BY MEXICO 1848

Colorado R.

Santa Fe

Las Vegas

Final Boundary 1850

DISPUTED BY U.S. AND MEXICO

Arkansas R.

Mississippi R.

Monterey

Stockton 1846

Santa Barbara

San Gabriel

Los Angeles

San Pasqual

San Diego

Kearny 1846

Gila R.

Socorro

El Brazio

El Paso del Norte

Doniphan 1847

Rio Grande

Pecos R.

Red R.

Sabine R.

TEXAS

Austin

San Antonio (The Alamo)

Corpus Christi

Scott 1846

New Orleans

Sloat 1846

Chihuahua

Wool

Nueces R.

Gulf of California

MEXICO

Saltillo

Buena Vista

Monterrey

Taylor 1846

Matamoros

American Blockade

Gulf of Mexico

PACIFIC OCEAN

Mazatlán

San Blas

Santa Ana 1847

San Luis Potosí

Tampico

Scott 1847

Cerro Gordo

Veracruz

Manzanillo

Mexico City

Chapultepec

PACIFIC OCEAN

Legend

- ★ American victory or occupation
- ✷ Mexican victory
- ■ Fort
- American forces
- Mexican forces
- ⬚⬚⬚ Blockade

0   250   500 mi
0   250   500 km

GROWTH OF THE UNITED STATES TO 1853

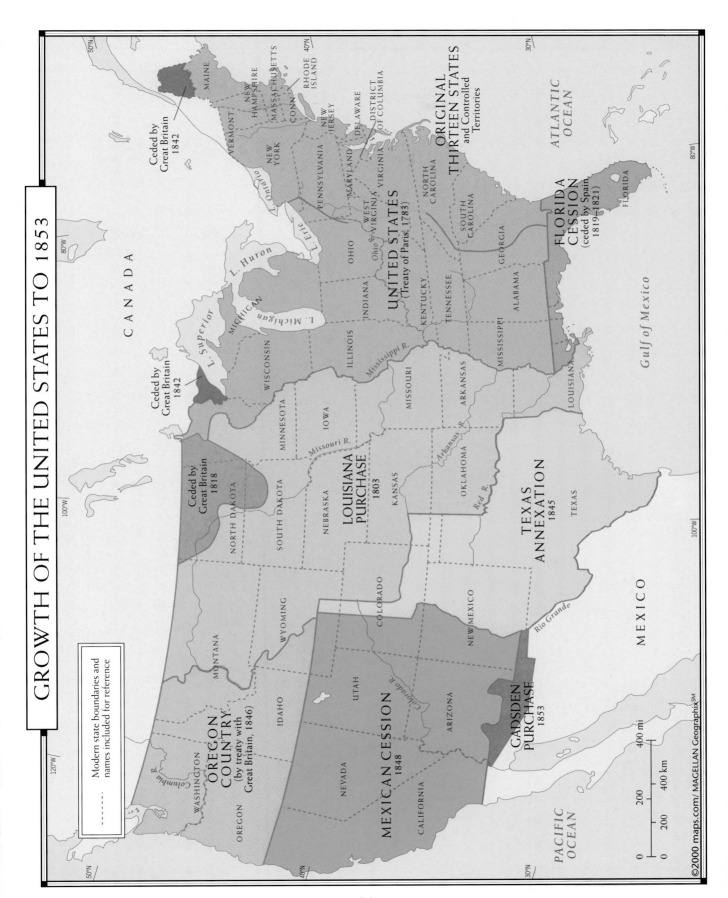

Modern state boundaries and names included for reference

CANADA

Ceded by Great Britain 1842

Ceded by Great Britain 1842

Ceded by Great Britain 1818

L. Ontario

L. Erie

L. Huron

L. Michigan

L. Superior

MAINE

VERMONT

NEW HAMPSHIRE

MASSACHUSETTS

RHODE ISLAND

CONN.

NEW YORK

NEW JERSEY

PENNSYLVANIA

DELAWARE

MARYLAND

DISTRICT OF COLUMBIA

WEST VIRGINIA

VIRGINIA

ORIGINAL THIRTEEN STATES and Controlled Territories

NORTH CAROLINA

SOUTH CAROLINA

GEORGIA

FLORIDA CESSION (ceded by Spain) 1819-1821

FLORIDA

ATLANTIC OCEAN

UNITED STATES (Treaty of Paris, 1783)

OHIO

Ohio R.

INDIANA

ILLINOIS

KENTUCKY

TENNESSEE

ALABAMA

MISSISSIPPI

LOUISIANA

Gulf of Mexico

MICHIGAN

WISCONSIN

MINNESOTA

IOWA

MISSOURI

Mississippi R.

Missouri R.

ARKANSAS

Arkansas R.

NORTH DAKOTA

SOUTH DAKOTA

NEBRASKA

LOUISIANA PURCHASE 1803

KANSAS

OKLAHOMA

Red R.

TEXAS ANNEXATION 1845

TEXAS

Rio Grande

MEXICO

MONTANA

WYOMING

COLORADO

NEW MEXICO

IDAHO

UTAH

ARIZONA

Colorado R.

GADSDEN PURCHASE 1853

OREGON COUNTRY (by treaty with Great Britain, 1846)

WASHINGTON

Columbia R.

OREGON

NEVADA

CALIFORNIA

MEXICAN CESSION 1848

PACIFIC OCEAN

400 mi

400 km

200

200

0

0

©2000 maps.com/ MAGELLAN Geographix℠

50°N

40°N

30°N

120°W

100°W

80°W

50°N

80°W

40°N

30°N

100°W

80°W

SLAVERY IN THE TERRITORIES, c. 1850–1854

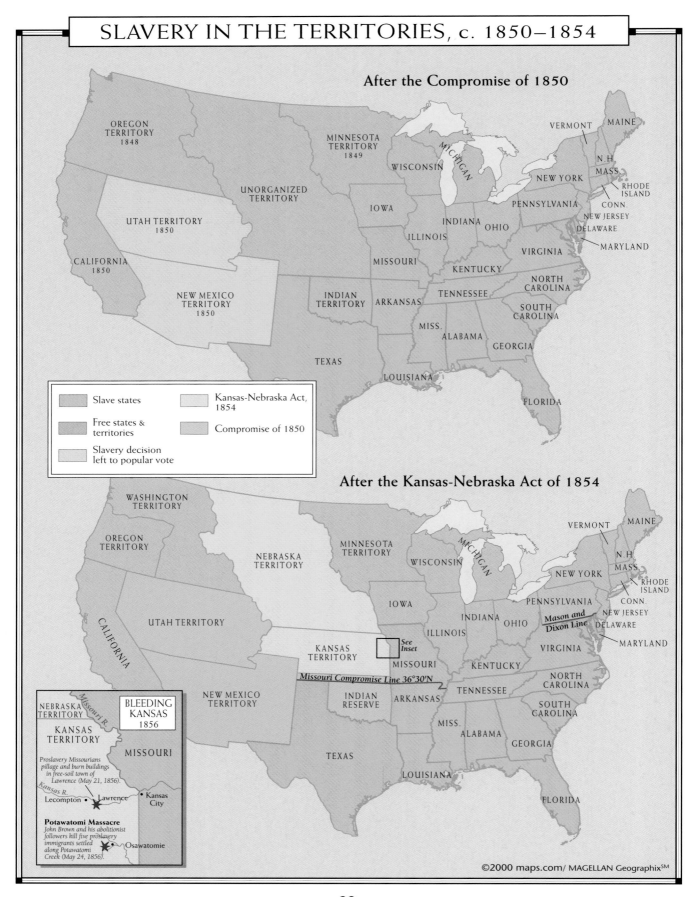

After the Compromise of 1850

OREGON TERRITORY 1848

MINNESOTA TERRITORY 1849

VERMONT

MAINE

WISCONSIN

MICHIGAN

N.H

UNORGANIZED TERRITORY

IOWA

NEW YORK

MASS

RHODE ISLAND

CONN.

UTAH TERRITORY 1850

PENNSYLVANIA

NEW JERSEY

INDIANA

OHIO

DELAWARE

ILLINOIS

MARYLAND

CALIFORNIA 1850

MISSOURI

VIRGINIA

KENTUCKY

NORTH CAROLINA

NEW MEXICO TERRITORY 1850

INDIAN TERRITORY

ARKANSAS

TENNESSEE

SOUTH CAROLINA

MISS.

ALABAMA

GEORGIA

TEXAS

LOUISIANA

FLORIDA

Legend
- Slave states
- Free states & territories
- Slavery decision left to popular vote
- Kansas-Nebraska Act, 1854
- Compromise of 1850

After the Kansas-Nebraska Act of 1854

WASHINGTON TERRITORY

OREGON TERRITORY

MINNESOTA TERRITORY

VERMONT

MAINE

NEBRASKA TERRITORY

WISCONSIN

MICHIGAN

N.H

IOWA

NEW YORK

MASS

RHODE ISLAND

UTAH TERRITORY

PENNSYLVANIA

CONN.

NEW JERSEY

INDIANA

OHIO

Mason and Dixon Line

DELAWARE

CALIFORNIA

ILLINOIS

VIRGINIA

MARYLAND

KANSAS TERRITORY

See Inset

MISSOURI

KENTUCKY

Missouri Compromise Line 36°30'N

NORTH CAROLINA

NEW MEXICO TERRITORY

INDIAN RESERVE

ARKANSAS

TENNESSEE

SOUTH CAROLINA

MISS.

ALABAMA

GEORGIA

TEXAS

LOUISIANA

FLORIDA

Inset
BLEEDING KANSAS 1856

NEBRASKA TERRITORY

Missouri R.

KANSAS TERRITORY

MISSOURI

Proslavery Missourians pillage and burn buildings in free-soil town of Lawrence (May 21, 1856).

Kansas R.

Lecompton • • Lawrence

• Kansas City

Potawatomi Massacre
John Brown and his abolitionist followers kill five proslavery immigrants settled along Potawatomi Creek (May 24, 1856).

★ • Osawatomie

©2000 maps.com/ MAGELLAN Geographix℠

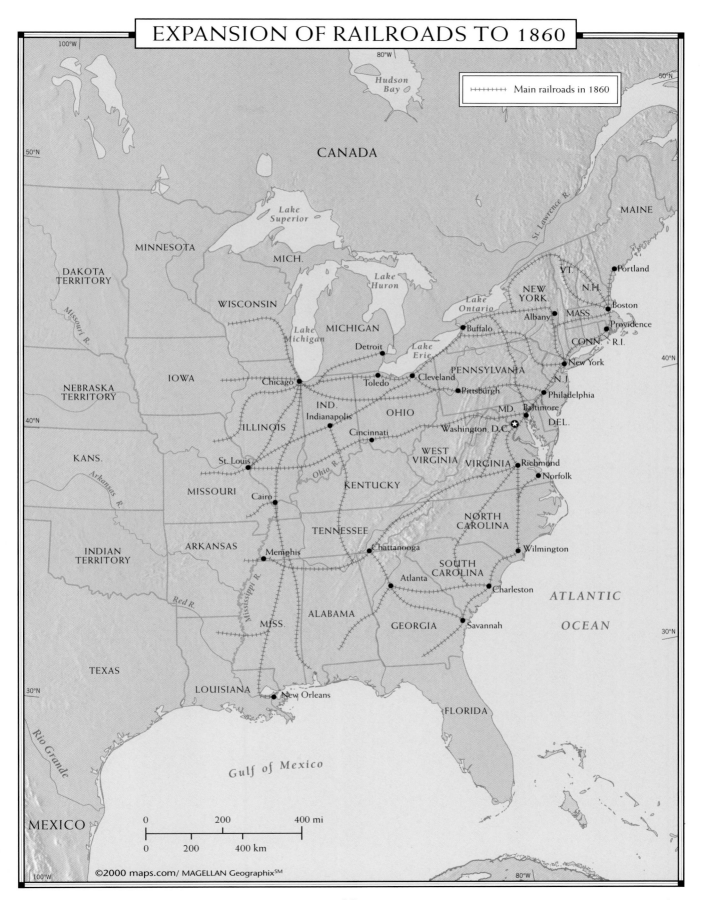

EXPANSION OF RAILROADS TO 1860

++++++++ Main railroads in 1860

©2000 maps.com/ MAGELLAN Geographix℠

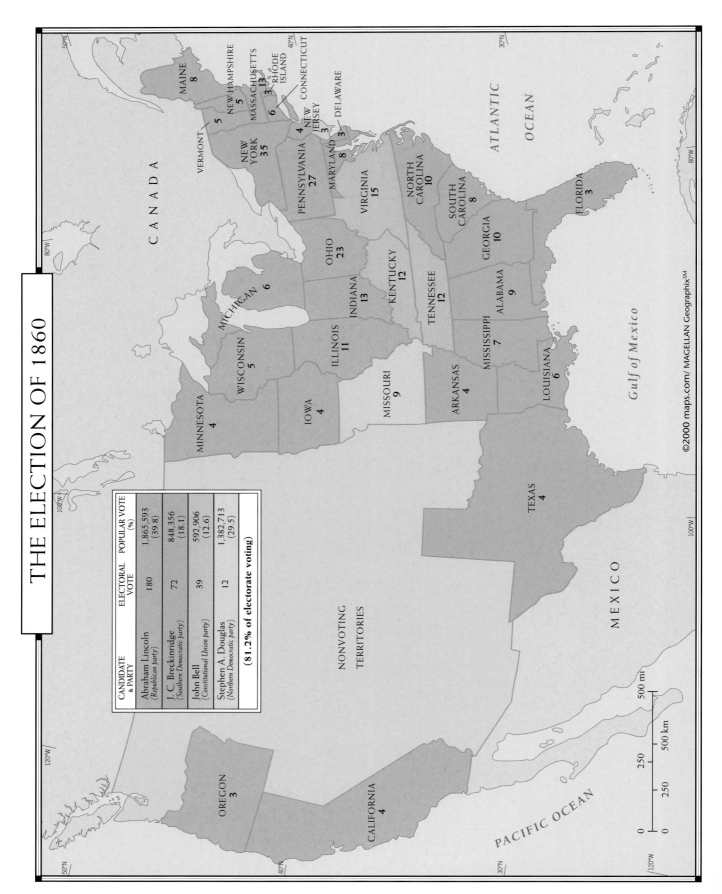

THE ELECTION OF 1860

CANDIDATE & PARTY	ELECTORAL VOTE	POPULAR VOTE (%)
Abraham Lincoln (Republican party)	180	1,865,593 (39.8)
J. C. Breckinridge (Southern Democratic party)	72	848,356 (18.1)
John Bell (Constitutional Union party)	39	592,906 (12.6)
Stephen A. Douglas (Northern Democratic party)	12	1,382,713 (29.5)

(81.2% of electorate voting)

CANADA

ATLANTIC OCEAN

MAINE 8

NEW HAMPSHIRE 5

MASSACHUSETTS 13

RHODE ISLAND 3

CONNECTICUT 6

VERMONT 5

NEW YORK 35

NEW JERSEY 4

DELAWARE 3

PENNSYLVANIA 27

MARYLAND 8

VIRGINIA 15

NORTH CAROLINA 10

SOUTH CAROLINA 8

FLORIDA 3

OHIO 23

KENTUCKY 12

GEORGIA 10

MICHIGAN 6

INDIANA 13

TENNESSEE 12

ALABAMA 9

ILLINOIS 11

WISCONSIN 5

MISSOURI 9

ARKANSAS 4

MISSISSIPPI 7

LOUISIANA 6

MINNESOTA 4

IOWA 4

Gulf of Mexico

TEXAS 4

MEXICO

NONVOTING TERRITORIES

OREGON 3

CALIFORNIA 4

PACIFIC OCEAN

0   250   500 mi

0   250   500 km

©2000 maps.com/ MAGELLAN Geographix℠

SECESSION OF THE SOUTHERN STATES, 1861

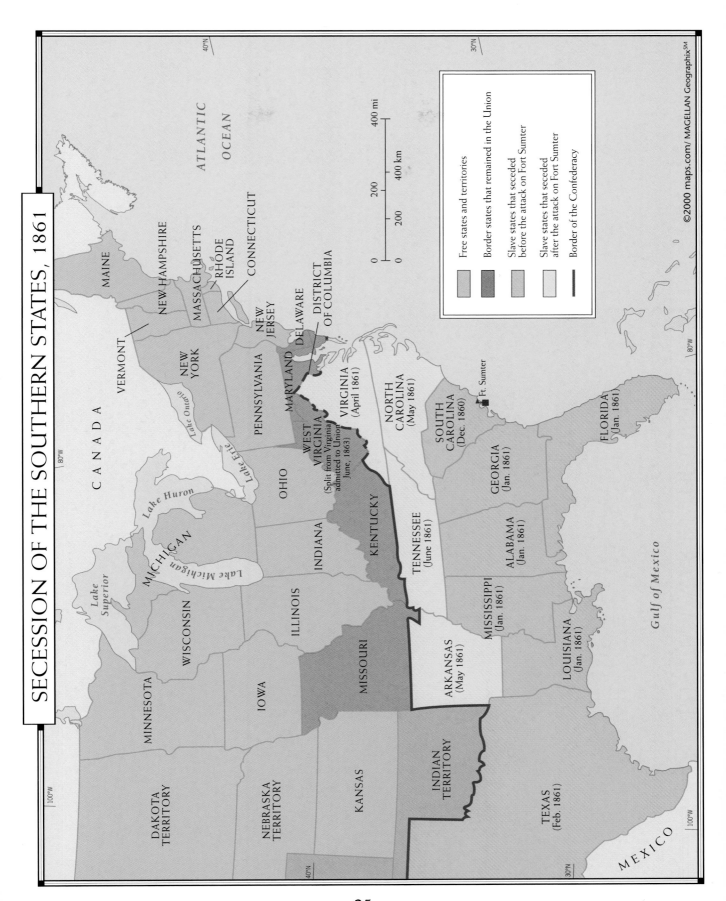

ATLANTIC OCEAN

CANADA

MAINE

VERMONT

NEW HAMPSHIRE

MASSACHUSETTS

RHODE ISLAND

CONNECTICUT

NEW YORK

NEW JERSEY

PENNSYLVANIA

DELAWARE

MARYLAND

DISTRICT OF COLUMBIA

Lake Ontario

Lake Erie

Lake Huron

Lake Superior

Lake Michigan

MICHIGAN

WISCONSIN

MINNESOTA

IOWA

ILLINOIS

INDIANA

OHIO

WEST VIRGINIA
(Split from Virginia admitted to Union June, 1863)

VIRGINIA
(April 1861)

KENTUCKY

NORTH CAROLINA
(May 1861)

SOUTH CAROLINA
(Dec. 1860)

TENNESSEE
(June 1861)

GEORGIA
(Jan. 1861)

ALABAMA
(Jan. 1861)

MISSISSIPPI
(Jan. 1861)

LOUISIANA
(Jan. 1861)

FLORIDA
(Jan. 1861)

Ft. Sumter

Gulf of Mexico

MISSOURI

ARKANSAS
(May 1861)

DAKOTA TERRITORY

NEBRASKA TERRITORY

KANSAS

INDIAN TERRITORY

TEXAS
(Feb. 1861)

MEXICO

40°N

30°N

80°W

100°W

400 mi

400 km

200

200

0

0

Free states and territories

Border states that remained in the Union

Slave states that seceded before the attack on Fort Sumter

Slave states that seceded after the attack on Fort Sumter

Border of the Confederacy

©2000 maps.com/ MAGELLAN Geographix℠

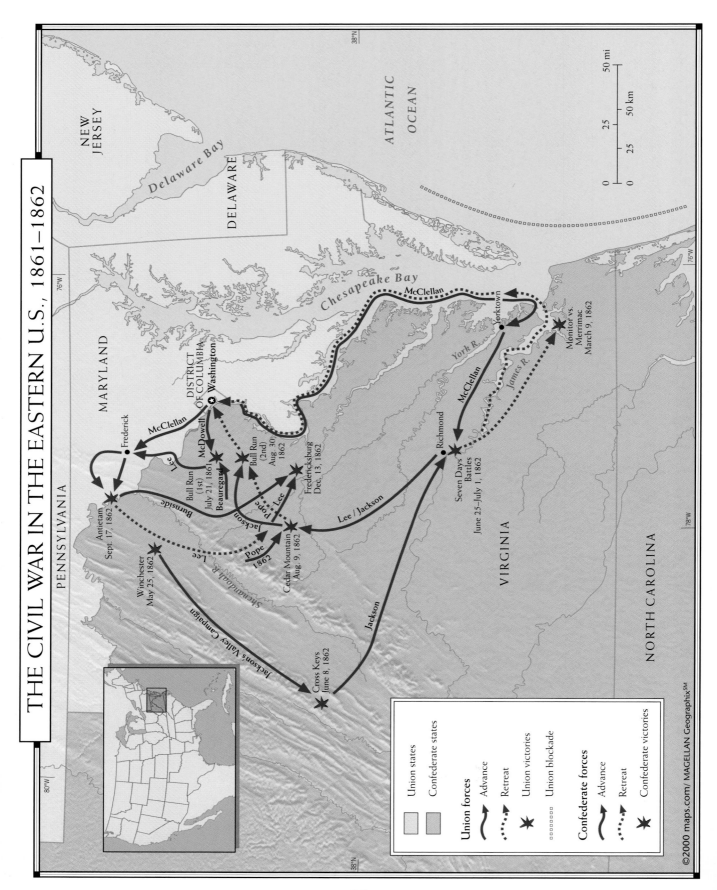

THE CIVIL WAR IN THE EASTERN U.S., 1861–1862

NEW JERSEY

Delaware Bay

DELAWARE

ATLANTIC OCEAN

50 mi
25 50 km
25
0 25
0

Chesapeake Bay

MARYLAND

McClellan

Yorktown

Monitor vs. Merrimac March 9, 1862

York R.

McClellan

James R.

DISTRICT OF COLUMBIA

Washington

Frederick

McClellan

McDowell

Lee

Bull Run (1st) July 21, 1861

Beauregard

Bull Run (2nd) Aug. 30, 1862

Fredericksburg Dec. 13, 1862

Richmond

Seven Days Battles June 25–July 1, 1862

PENNSYLVANIA

Antietam Sept. 17, 1862

Burnside

Jackson

Pope

Lee

Cedar Mountain Aug. 9, 1862

Lee / Jackson

Lee 1862

Pope 1862

Shenandoah R.

VIRGINIA

Winchester May 25, 1862

Jackson's Valley Campaign

Jackson

Cross Keys June 8, 1862

NORTH CAROLINA

Union forces

Union states
Confederate states

Union forces
Advance
Retreat
Union victories
Union blockade

Confederate forces
Advance
Retreat
Confederate victories

80°W   76°W   38°N   76°W   78°N   38°N

THE CIVIL WAR IN THE CENTRAL U.S., 1862–1863

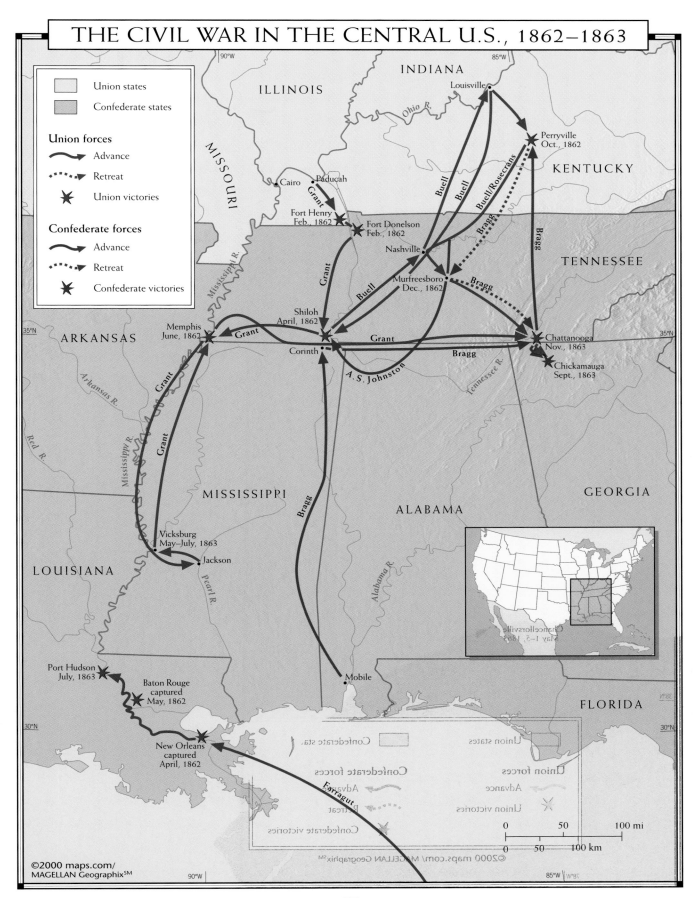

Legend:

Union states
Confederate states

Union forces
— Advance
┅► Retreat
★ Union victories

Confederate forces
— Advance
┅► Retreat
★ Confederate victories

Labels on map:

ILLINOIS · INDIANA · MISSOURI · KENTUCKY · TENNESSEE · ARKANSAS · MISSISSIPPI · ALABAMA · GEORGIA · LOUISIANA · FLORIDA

Cairo · Paducah · Louisville · Perryville Oct., 1862 · Fort Henry Feb., 1862 · Fort Donelson Feb., 1862 · Nashville · Murfreesboro Dec., 1862 · Memphis June, 1862 · Shiloh April, 1862 · Corinth · Chattanooga Nov., 1863 · Chickamauga Sept., 1863 · Vicksburg May–July, 1863 · Jackson · Port Hudson July, 1863 · Baton Rouge captured May, 1862 · New Orleans captured April, 1862 · Mobile

Grant · Buell · Buell/Rosecrans · Bragg · A. S. Johnston · Farragut

Ohio R. · Mississippi R. · Arkansas R. · Red R. · Pearl R. · Tennessee R. · Alabama R.

90°W · 85°W · 35°N · 30°N · 38°N

0   50   100 mi
0   50   100 km

©2000 maps.com/
MAGELLAN Geographix℠

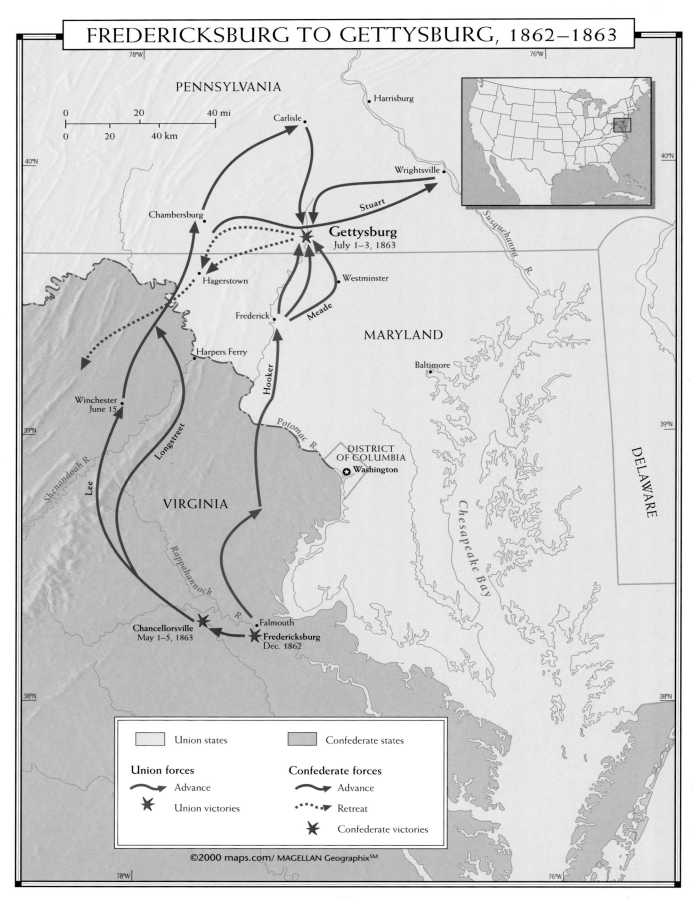

PENNSYLVANIA

Harrisburg

Carlisle

Wrightsville

Stuart

Chambersburg

Gettysburg
July 1–3, 1863

Hagerstown

Westminster

Frederick

Meade

MARYLAND

Harpers Ferry

Hooker

Baltimore

Winchester
June 15

Longstreet

Shenandoah R.

Lee

Rappahannock

Potomac R.

DISTRICT
OF COLUMBIA
✪ Washington

VIRGINIA

DELAWARE

Chesapeake Bay

R.

Falmouth

Chancellorsville
May 1–5, 1863

Fredericksburg
Dec. 1862

Susquehanna R.

0   20   40 mi
0   20   40 km

78°W   76°W

40°N

39°N

38°N

Legend:

| | Union states | | Confederate states |

Union forces
Advance
Union victories

Confederate forces
Advance
Retreat
Confederate victories

©2000 maps.com/ MAGELLAN Geographix℠

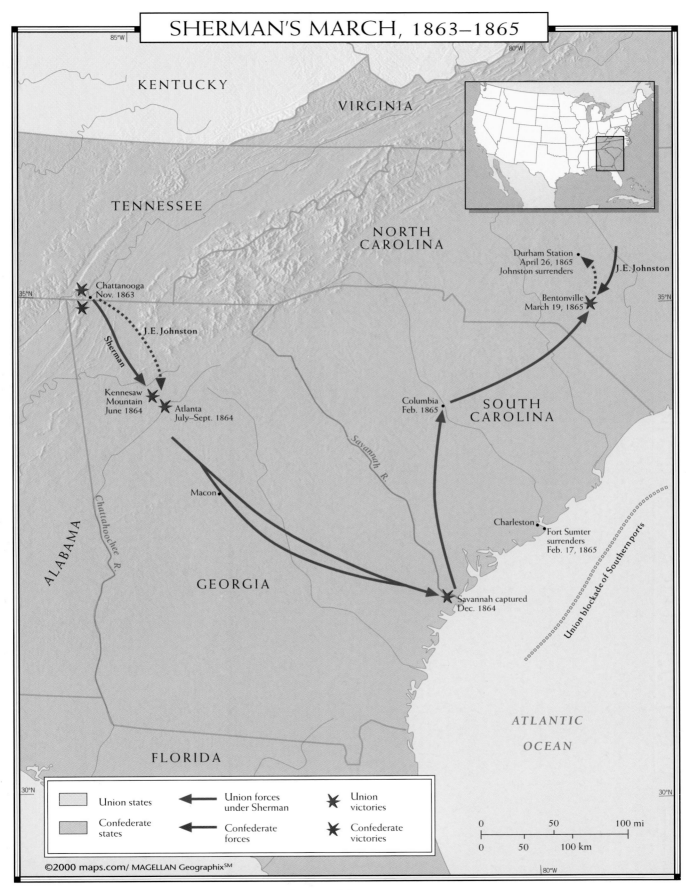

SHERMAN'S MARCH, 1863–1865

KENTUCKY

VIRGINIA

TENNESSEE

NORTH CAROLINA

Durham Station
April 26, 1865
Johnston surrenders

J.E. Johnston

Chattanooga
Nov. 1863

Bentonville
March 19, 1865

35°N

J.E. Johnston

Sherman

Columbia
Feb. 1865

SOUTH CAROLINA

Kennesaw
Mountain
June 1864

Atlanta
July–Sept. 1864

Savannah R.

Macon

Charleston

Fort Sumter
surrenders
Feb. 17, 1865

Union blockade of Southern ports

ALABAMA

Chattahoochee R.

GEORGIA

Savannah captured
Dec. 1864

FLORIDA

ATLANTIC OCEAN

30°N

Legend:

Union states	Union forces under Sherman	Union victories
Confederate states	Confederate forces	Confederate victories

0   50   100 mi
0   50   100 km

©2000 maps.com/ MAGELLAN Geographix℠

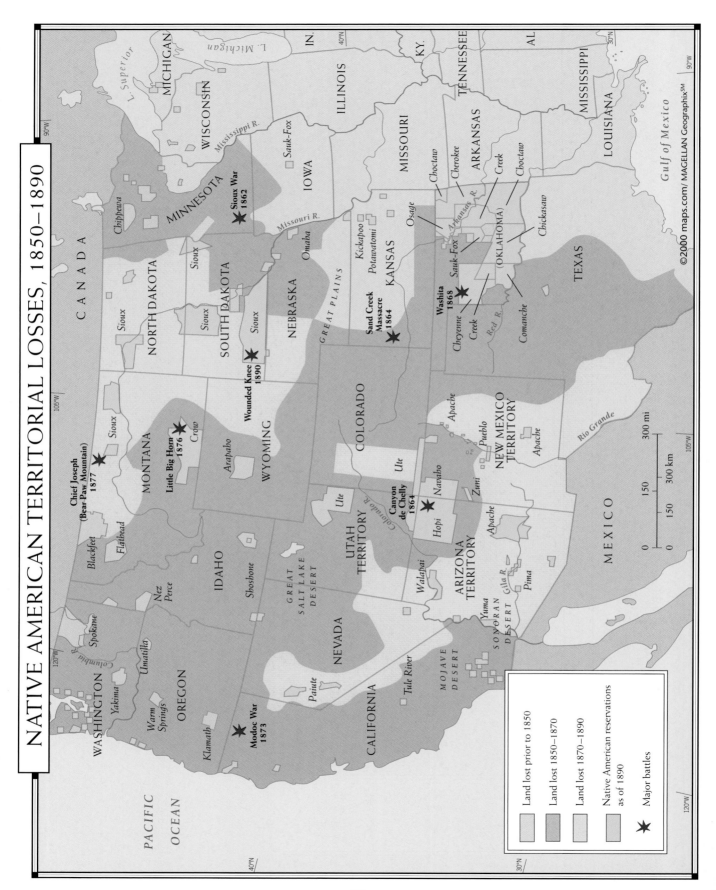

NATIVE AMERICAN TERRITORIAL LOSSES, 1850–1890

©2000 maps.com/ MAGELLAN Geographix℠

CANADA

MICHIGAN
L. Superior
L. Michigan
IN.
WISCONSIN
Mississippi R.
Chippewa
MINNESOTA
Sioux War 1862
Sioux
NORTH DAKOTA
SOUTH DAKOTA
Sioux
Sioux
Sioux
Wounded Knee 1890
Missouri R.
Omaha
NEBRASKA
GREAT PLAINS
Kickapoo
Potawatomi
Sauk-Fox
IOWA
Osage
KANSAS
Sand Creek Massacre 1864
MISSOURI
ILLINOIS
KY.
TENNESSEE
AL.
ARKANSAS
MISSISSIPPI
LOUISIANA
Gulf of Mexico
Choctaw
Cherokee
Creek
Choctaw
(OKLAHOMA)
Chickasaw
Arkansas R.
Sauk-Fox
Washita 1868
Cheyenne
Creek
Red R.
Comanche
TEXAS

Sauk-Fox

Sioux
Chief Joseph (Bear Paw Mountain) 1877
Little Big Horn 1876
Crow
MONTANA
Arapaho
WYOMING
COLORADO
Ute
Apache
Pueblo
NEW MEXICO TERRITORY
Apache
Rio Grande
Zuni
Navaho
Canyon de Chelly 1864
Hopi
Colorado R.
Ute
UTAH TERRITORY
Apache
ARIZONA TERRITORY
Walapai
Gila R.
Pima
Yuma
SONORAN DESERT
MEXICO

Blackfeet
Flathead
IDAHO
Shoshone
GREAT SALT LAKE DESERT
NEVADA
Nez Perce
Spokane
Umatilla
Columbia R.
Yakima
Warm Springs
WASHINGTON
OREGON
Klamath
Modoc War 1873
Paiute
Tule River
CALIFORNIA
MOJAVE DESERT

PACIFIC OCEAN

90°W
105°W
120°W
40°N
30°N
120°W
105°W
90°W
40°N
30°N

300 mi
300 km
150
150
0
0

Legend

- Land lost prior to 1850
- Land lost 1850–1870
- Land lost 1870–1890
- Native American reservations as of 1890
- ★ Major battles

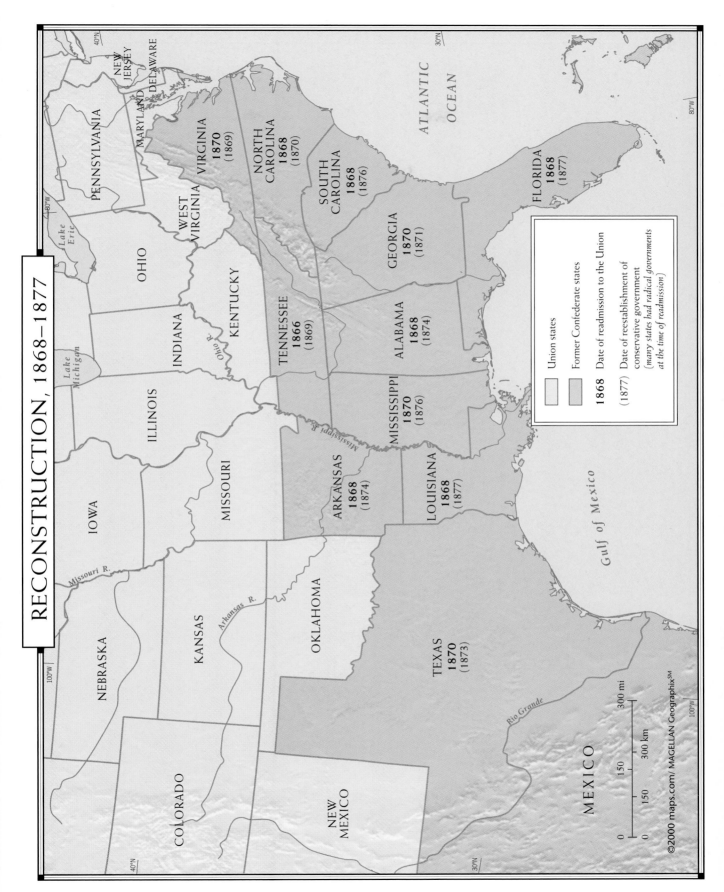

RECONSTRUCTION, 1868–1877

NEW JERSEY

DELAWARE

MARYLAND

PENNSYLVANIA

ATLANTIC OCEAN

40°N

30°N

80°W

VIRGINIA
1870
(1869)

NORTH CAROLINA
1868
(1870)

SOUTH CAROLINA
1868
(1876)

FLORIDA
1868
(1877)

WEST VIRGINIA

OHIO

KENTUCKY

GEORGIA
1870
(1871)

Lake Erie

80°W

TENNESSEE
1866
(1869)

ALABAMA
1868
(1874)

INDIANA

ILLINOIS

Lake Michigan

Ohio R.

Mississippi R.

MISSISSIPPI
1870
(1876)

IOWA

MISSOURI

Missouri R.

Arkansas R.

ARKANSAS
1868
(1874)

LOUISIANA
1868
(1877)

Gulf of Mexico

NEBRASKA

KANSAS

OKLAHOMA

TEXAS
1870
(1873)

COLORADO

NEW MEXICO

Rio Grande

MEXICO

100°W

100°W

40°N

30°N

	Union states
	Former Confederate states
1868	Date of readmission to the Union
(1877)	Date of reestablishment of conservative government (*many states had radical governments at the time of readmission*)

0   150   300 mi

0   150   300 km

©2000 maps.com/ MAGELLAN Geographix℠

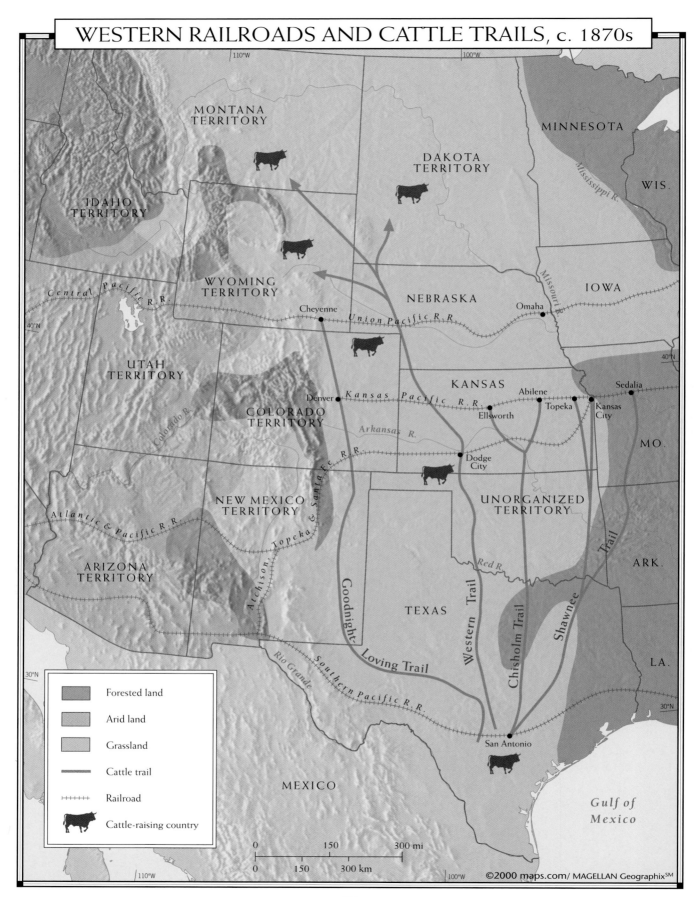

WESTERN RAILROADS AND CATTLE TRAILS, c. 1870s

MONTANA
TERRITORY

DAKOTA
TERRITORY

MINNESOTA

WIS.

IDAHO
TERRITORY

Central Pacific R. R.

WYOMING
TERRITORY

NEBRASKA

IOWA

Omaha

Missouri R.

Cheyenne

Union Pacific R. R.

UTAH
TERRITORY

KANSAS

Sedalia

Denver

Kansas Pacific R. R.

Abilene

Kansas City

Topeka

COLORADO
TERRITORY

Ellsworth

Arkansas R.

MO.

Colorado R.

Dodge
City

Atlantic & Pacific R. R.

NEW MEXICO
TERRITORY

UNORGANIZED
TERRITORY

ARK.

ARIZONA
TERRITORY

Atchison, Topeka & Santa Fe R. R.

Red R.

Western Trail

Chisholm Trail

Shawnee Trail

LA.

Rio Grande

Goodnight-Loving Trail

Southern Pacific R. R.

TEXAS

San Antonio

MEXICO

Gulf of
Mexico

Legend
- Forested land
- Arid land
- Grassland
- —— Cattle trail
- +++++ Railroad
- Cattle-raising country

| 0 | 150 | 300 mi |
| 0 | 150 | 300 km |

©2000 maps.com/ MAGELLAN Geographix℠

IMMIGRANTS TO THE UNITED STATES, 1890

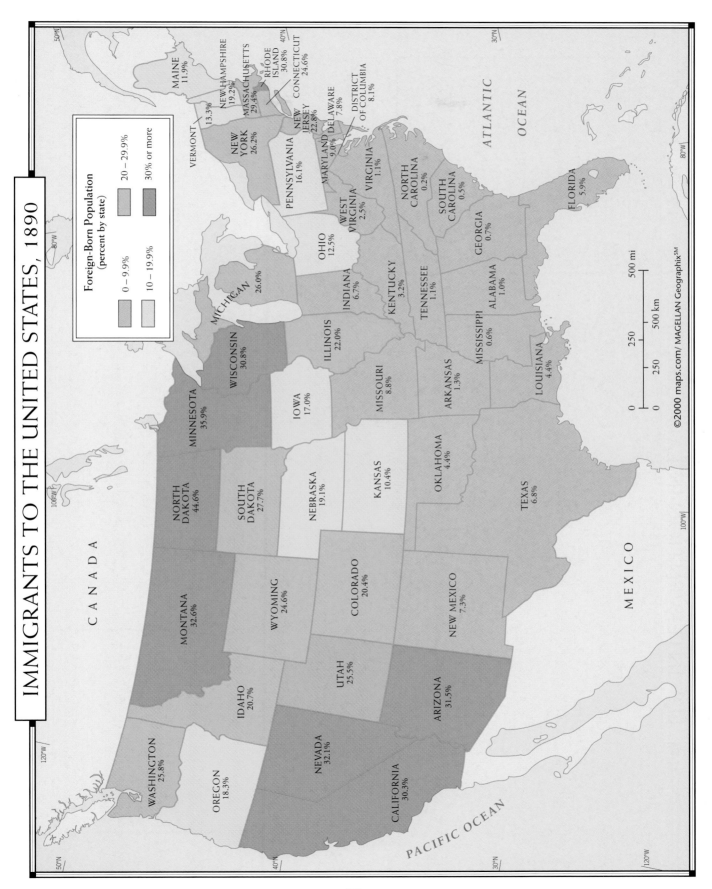

Foreign-Born Population
(percent by state)

- 0 – 9.9%
- 10 – 19.9%
- 20 – 29.9%
- 30% or more

MAINE 11.9%
NEW HAMPSHIRE 19.2%
VERMONT 13.3%
MASSACHUSETTS 29.4%
RHODE ISLAND 30.8%
CONNECTICUT 24.6%
NEW YORK 26.2%
NEW JERSEY 22.8%
PENNSYLVANIA 16.1%
DELAWARE 7.8%
MARYLAND 9.0%
DISTRICT OF COLUMBIA 8.1%
WEST VIRGINIA 2.5%
VIRGINIA 1.1%
NORTH CAROLINA 0.2%
SOUTH CAROLINA 0.5%
GEORGIA 0.7%
FLORIDA 5.9%
OHIO 12.5%
MICHIGAN 26.0%
INDIANA 6.7%
KENTUCKY 3.2%
TENNESSEE 1.1%
ALABAMA 1.0%
MISSISSIPPI 0.6%
LOUISIANA 4.4%
ILLINOIS 22.0%
WISCONSIN 30.8%
MINNESOTA 35.9%
IOWA 17.0%
MISSOURI 8.8%
ARKANSAS 1.3%
OKLAHOMA 4.4%
NORTH DAKOTA 44.6%
SOUTH DAKOTA 27.7%
NEBRASKA 19.1%
KANSAS 10.4%
TEXAS 6.8%
MONTANA 32.6%
WYOMING 24.6%
COLORADO 20.4%
NEW MEXICO 7.3%
IDAHO 20.7%
UTAH 25.5%
ARIZONA 31.5%
WASHINGTON 25.8%
OREGON 18.3%
NEVADA 32.1%
CALIFORNIA 30.3%

CANADA

MEXICO

ATLANTIC OCEAN

PACIFIC OCEAN

500 mi
250
0
500 km
250
0

©2000 maps.com/ MAGELLAN Geographix℠

50°N
40°N
30°N
120°W
110°W
100°W
90°W
80°W

U.S. INTERVENTION IN LATIN AMERICA, 1895–1940s

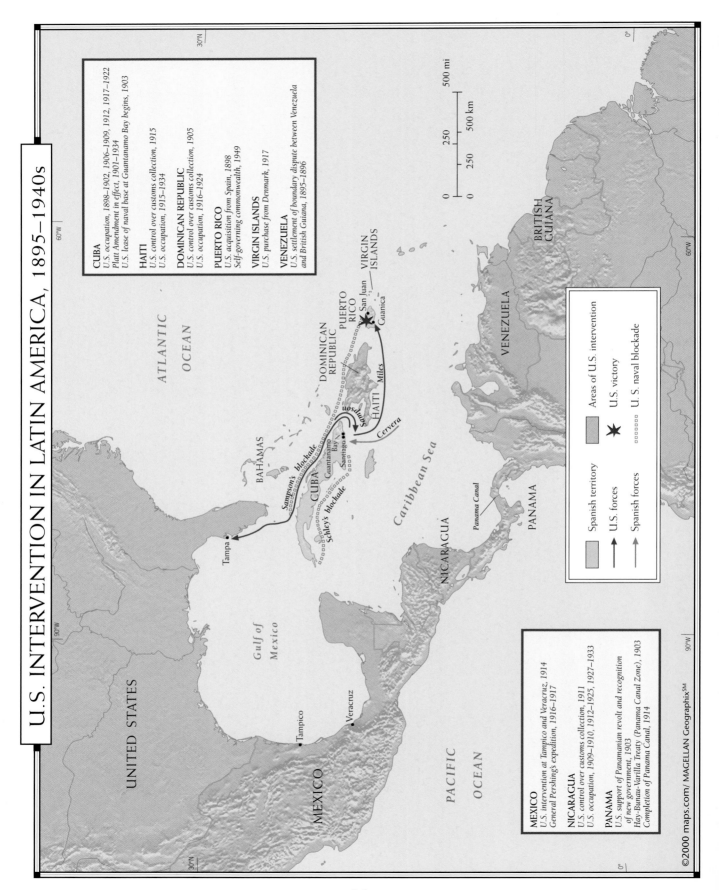

CUBA
U.S. occupation, 1898–1902, 1906–1909, 1912, 1917–1922
Platt Amendment in effect, 1901–1934
U.S. lease of naval base at Guantanamo Bay begins, 1903

HAITI
U.S. control over customs collection, 1915
U.S. occupation, 1915–1934

DOMINICAN REPUBLIC
U.S. control over customs collection, 1905
U.S. occupation, 1916–1924

PUERTO RICO
U.S. acquisition from Spain, 1898
Self-governing commonwealth, 1949

VIRGIN ISLANDS
U.S. purchase from Denmark, 1917

VENEZUELA
U.S. settlement of boundary dispute between Venezuela and British Guiana, 1895–1896

MEXICO
U.S. intervention at Tampico and Veracruz, 1914
General Pershing's expedition, 1916–1917

NICARAGUA
U.S. control over customs collection, 1911
U.S. occupation, 1909–1910, 1912–1925, 1927–1933

PANAMA
U.S. support of Panamanian revolt and recognition of new government, 1903
Hay-Bunau-Varilla Treaty (Panama Canal Zone), 1903
Completion of Panama Canal, 1914

Spanish territory
Areas of U.S. intervention
U.S. forces
U.S. victory
Spanish forces
U. S. naval blockade

UNITED STATES
ATLANTIC OCEAN
Gulf of Mexico
Tampa
Tampico
Veracruz
MEXICO
BAHAMAS
CUBA
Guantanamo Bay
Santiago
Sampson's blockade
Schley's blockade
Cervera
Sampson
Miles
HAITI
DOMINICAN REPUBLIC
PUERTO RICO
San Juan
Guanica
VIRGIN ISLANDS
Caribbean Sea
NICARAGUA
PANAMA
Panama Canal
VENEZUELA
BRITISH GUIANA
PACIFIC OCEAN

500 mi
500 km
0   250   500
0   250

©2000 maps.com/ MAGELLAN Geographix℠

U.S. TERRITORY AND LEASES, 1857–1903

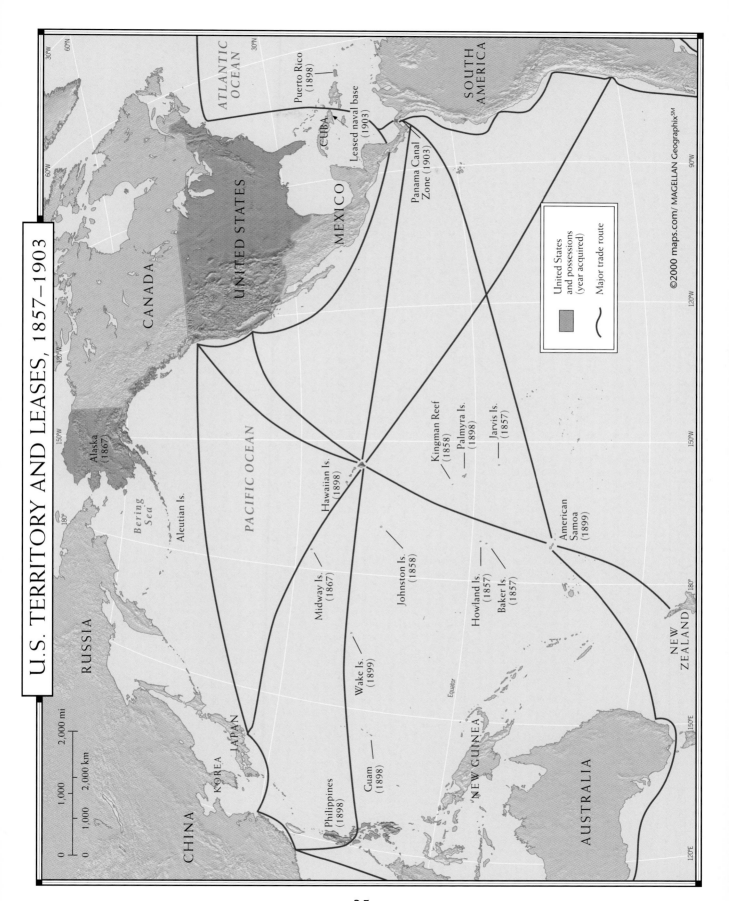

CANADA

UNITED STATES

ATLANTIC OCEAN

SOUTH AMERICA

MEXICO

Puerto Rico (1898)

CUBA

Leased naval base (1903)

Panama Canal Zone (1903)

RUSSIA

Alaska (1867)

Bering Sea

Aleutian Is.

PACIFIC OCEAN

Hawaiian Is. (1898)

Kingman Reef (1858)

Palmyra Is. (1898)

Jarvis Is. (1857)

American Samoa (1899)

Midway Is. (1867)

Johnston Is. (1858)

Howland Is. (1857)

Baker Is. (1857)

CHINA

KOREA

JAPAN

Wake Is. (1899)

Philippines (1898)

Guam (1898)

Equator

NEW GUINEA

AUSTRALIA

NEW ZEALAND

United States and possessions (year acquired)

Major trade route

©2000 maps.com/ MAGELLAN Geographix℠

2,000 mi

2,000 km

1,000

1,000

0

0

WOMAN'S SUFFRAGE BEFORE THE 19th AMENDMENT

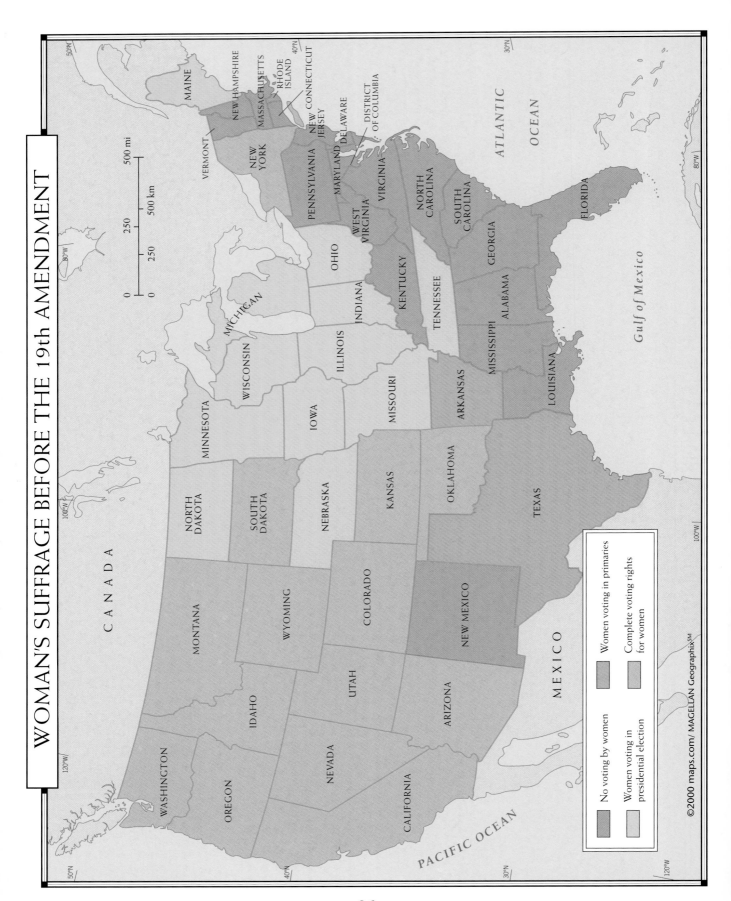

Legend:
- No voting by women
- Women voting in presidential election
- Women voting in primaries
- Complete voting rights for women

©2000 maps.com/ MAGELLAN Geographix℠

WORLD WAR I IN EUROPE

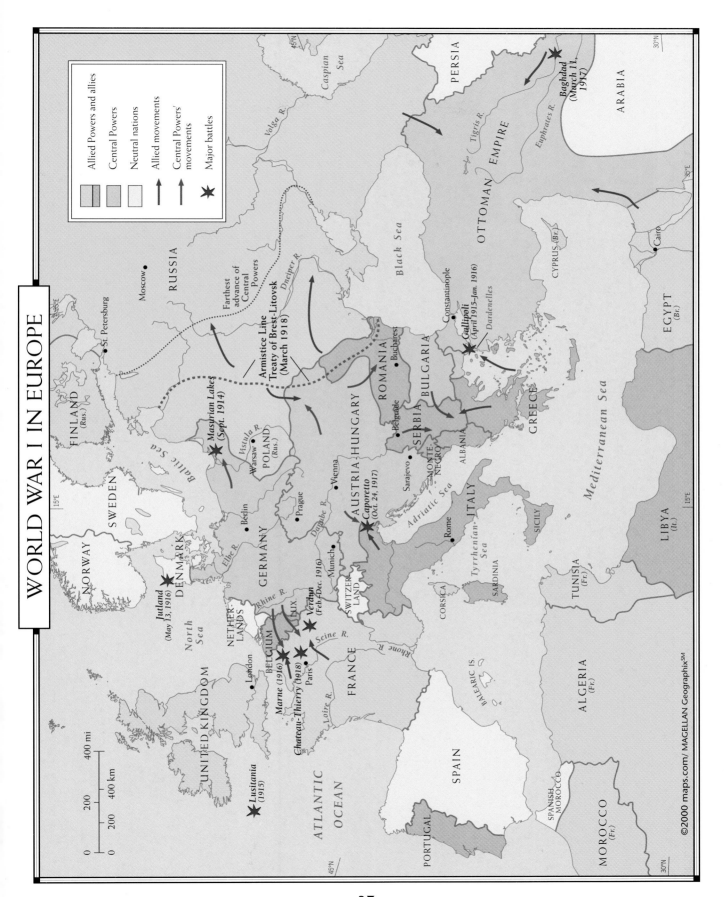

Legend:

Allied Powers and allies
Central Powers
Neutral nations
Allied movements
Central Powers' movements
Major battles

Moscow

St. Petersburg

FINLAND (Rus.)

RUSSIA

Farthest advance of Central Powers

Armistice Line Treaty of Brest-Litovsk (March 1918)

Masurian Lakes (Sept. 1914)

Warsaw

POLAND (Rus.)

Vistula R.

Dnieper R.

Volga R.

Caspian Sea

PERSIA

ARABIA

Baghdad (March 11, 1917)

OTTOMAN EMPIRE

Tigris R.

Euphrates R.

Black Sea

Constantinople

Gallipoli (April 1915–Jan. 1916)

Dardanelles

CYPRUS (Br.)

Cairo

EGYPT (Br.)

Bucharest

ROMANIA

SERBIA

BULGARIA

Belgrade

MONTE-NEGRO

ALBANIA

GREECE

Sarajevo

AUSTRIA-HUNGARY

Vienna

Caporetto (Oct. 24, 1917)

Danube R.

Prague

Berlin

Elbe R.

GERMANY

Munich

SWITZERLAND

ITALY

Rome

Adriatic Sea

Tyrrhenian Sea

SARDINIA

CORSICA

SICILY

Mediterranean Sea

LIBYA (It.)

SWEDEN

NORWAY

DENMARK

Jutland (May 13, 1916)

North Sea

Baltic Sea

NETHERLANDS

BELGIUM

Rhine R.

LUX.

Verdun (Feb.–Dec. 1916)

Marne (1916)

Chateau-Thierry (1918)

Paris

Seine R.

FRANCE

Loire R.

Rhône R.

London

UNITED KINGDOM

Lusitania (1915)

ATLANTIC OCEAN

SPAIN

PORTUGAL

BALEARIC IS.

SPANISH MOROCCO

MOROCCO (Fr.)

ALGERIA (Fr.)

TUNISIA (Fr.)

400 mi

400 km

0   200   400

45°N

30°N

15°E

©2000 maps.com/ MAGELLAN Geographix℠

U.S. PARTICIPATION ON THE WESTERN FRONT, 1918

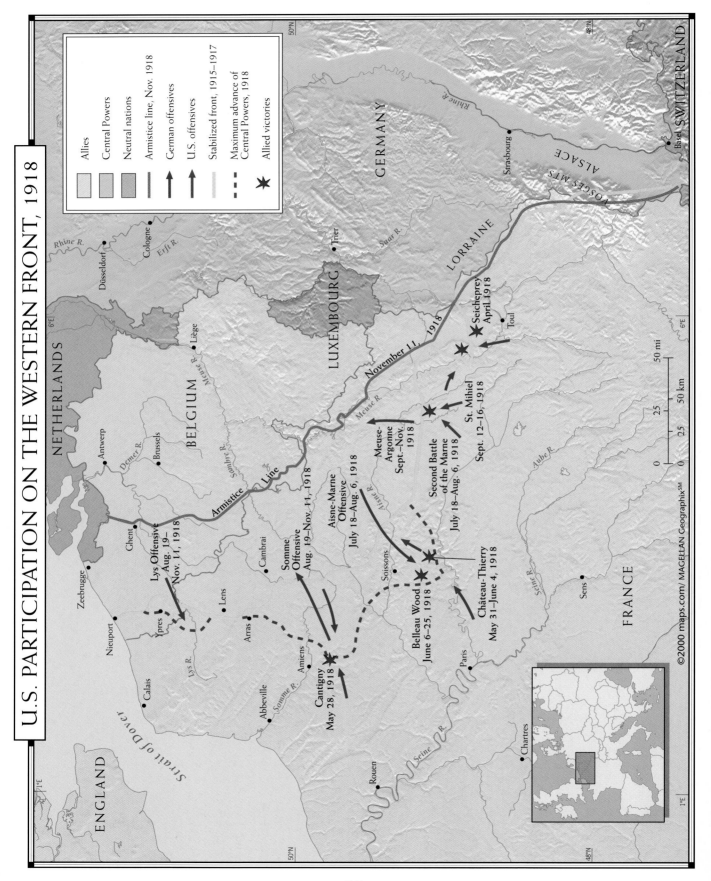

Legend:
- Allies
- Central Powers
- Neutral nations
- Armistice line, Nov. 1918
- German offensives
- U.S. offensives
- Stabilized front, 1915–1917
- Maximum advance of Central Powers, 1918
- Allied victories

ENGLAND

Strait of Dover

NETHERLANDS

Antwerp
Brussels
BELGIUM
Ghent
Zeebrugge
Nieuport
Calais
Ypres
Abbeville
Arras
Lens
Cambrai
Amiens
Rouen
Chartres

Rhine R.
Düsseldorf
Cologne
Erft R.

GERMANY

Liège
Trier
Saar R.
LUXEMBOURG

Meuse R.

Rhine R.
Strasbourg
ALSACE
VOSGES MTS.
Basel SWITZERLAND

LORRAINE

November 11, 1918

Seicheprey
April 1918
Toul

St. Mihiel
Sept. 12–16, 1918

Meuse-
Argonne
Sept.–Nov.
1918

Second Battle
of the Marne
July 18–Aug. 6, 1918

Aisne-Marne
Offensive
July 18–Aug. 6, 1918

Soissons

Belleau Wood
June 6–25, 1918

Château-Thierry
May 31–June 4, 1918

Paris

Aube R.

Sens

Seine R.

FRANCE

Armistice Line

Lys Offensive
Aug. 19–
Nov. 11, 1918

Somme
Offensive
Aug. 19–Nov. 11, 1918

Cantigny
May 28, 1918

Lys R.
Somme R.
Seine R.

Demer R.
Sambre R.
Aisne R.

©2000 maps.com/ MAGELLAN GeographixSM

50 mi
50 km
0   25   25   50

— 38 —

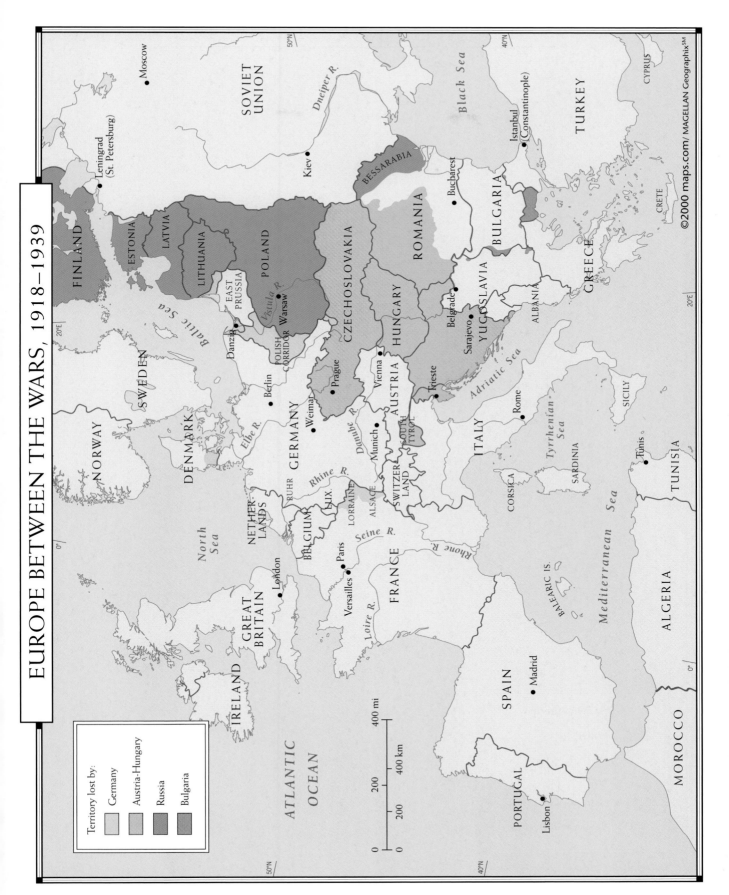

EUROPE BETWEEN THE WARS, 1918–1939

Territory lost by:
- Germany
- Austria-Hungary
- Russia
- Bulgaria

©2000 maps.com/MAGELLAN Geographix℠

ATLANTIC OCEAN

North Sea

IRELAND

GREAT BRITAIN

London

NORWAY

SWEDEN

DENMARK

NETHER-LANDS

BELGIUM

Lux.

FRANCE

Paris

Versailles

Seine R.

Loire R.

Rhône R.

RUHR

Rhine R.

Elbe R.

GERMANY

Berlin

Weimar

Munich

LORRAINE

ALSACE

SWITZER-LAND

SOUTH TYROL

ITALY

Rome

CORSICA

SARDINIA

Tyrrhenian Sea

Mediterranean Sea

BALEARIC IS.

SPAIN

Madrid

PORTUGAL

Lisbon

MOROCCO

ALGERIA

TUNISIA

Tunis

SICILY

Baltic Sea

FINLAND

Leningrad (St. Petersburg)

ESTONIA

LATVIA

LITHUANIA

EAST PRUSSIA

Danzig

POLISH CORRIDOR

POLAND

Warsaw

Vistula R.

Prague

CZECHOSLOVAKIA

Vienna

AUSTRIA

Danube R.

HUNGARY

Trieste

Adriatic Sea

YUGOSLAVIA

Belgrade

Sarajevo

ALBANIA

SOVIET UNION

Moscow

Kiev

Dneiper R.

BESSARABIA

ROMANIA

Bucharest

BULGARIA

Black Sea

GREECE

TURKEY

Istanbul (Constantinople)

CRETE

CYPRUS

50°N

40°N

20°E

0°

400 mi

400 km

200

200

0

0

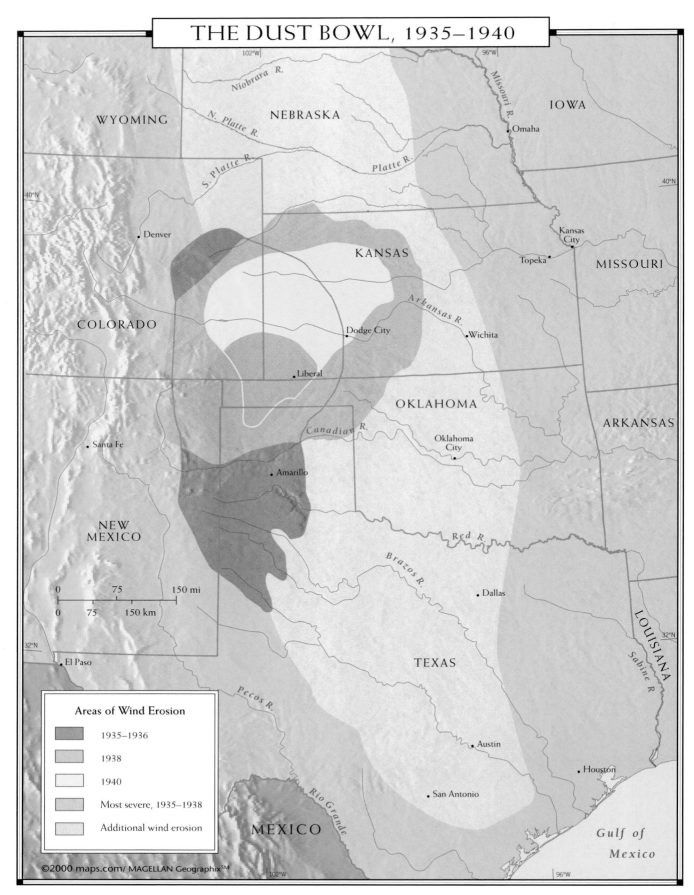

WYOMING

NEBRASKA

Niobrara R.

N. Platte R.

S. Platte R.

Platte R.

IOWA

Missouri R.

Omaha

40°N

40°N

Denver

KANSAS

Kansas City

Topeka

MISSOURI

COLORADO

Dodge City

Arkansas R.

Wichita

Liberal

OKLAHOMA

ARKANSAS

Canadian R.

Oklahoma City

Santa Fe

Amarillo

NEW MEXICO

Red R.

Brazos R.

0   75   150 mi

0   75   150 km

Dallas

LOUISIANA

32°N

El Paso

TEXAS

Sabine R.

Areas of Wind Erosion

1935–1936

1938

1940

Most severe, 1935–1938

Additional wind erosion

Austin

Houston

Pecos R.

San Antonio

Rio Grande

MEXICO

Gulf of Mexico

©2000 maps.com/ MAGELLAN Geographix℠

102°W

96°W

WORLD WAR II IN EUROPE, 1940–1945

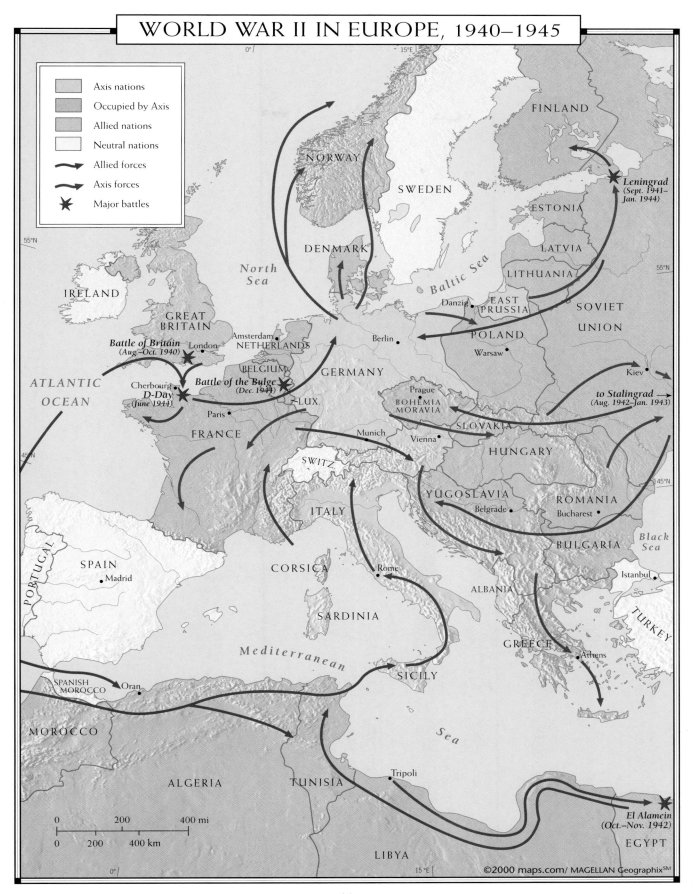

Legend:
- Axis nations
- Occupied by Axis
- Allied nations
- Neutral nations
- Allied forces
- Axis forces
- Major battles

Leningrad (Sept. 1941–Jan. 1944)

Battle of Britain (Aug.–Oct. 1940)

Battle of the Bulge (Dec. 1944)

D-Day (June 1944)

to Stalingrad → (Aug. 1942–Jan. 1943)

El Alamein (Oct.–Nov. 1942)

FINLAND, NORWAY, SWEDEN, DENMARK, ESTONIA, LATVIA, LITHUANIA, EAST PRUSSIA, POLAND, SOVIET UNION, IRELAND, GREAT BRITAIN, NETHERLANDS, BELGIUM, GERMANY, FRANCE, SWITZ., ITALY, BOHEMIA MORAVIA, SLOVAKIA, HUNGARY, YUGOSLAVIA, ROMANIA, BULGARIA, ALBANIA, GREECE, TURKEY, PORTUGAL, SPAIN, CORSICA, SARDINIA, SICILY, SPANISH MOROCCO, MOROCCO, ALGERIA, TUNISIA, LIBYA, EGYPT

North Sea, Baltic Sea, ATLANTIC OCEAN, Mediterranean Sea, Black Sea

London, Amsterdam, Cherbourg, Paris, LUX., Munich, Vienna, Prague, Berlin, Danzig, Warsaw, Kiev, Belgrade, Bucharest, Istanbul, Athens, Rome, Madrid, Oran, Tripoli

©2000 maps.com/ MAGELLAN Geographix℠

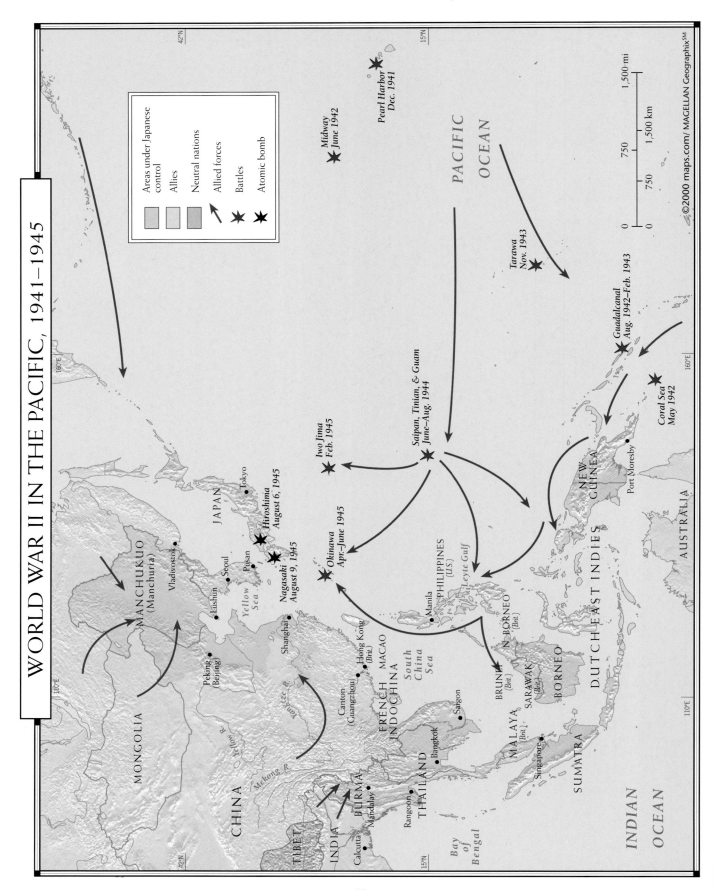

WORLD WAR II IN THE PACIFIC, 1941–1945

Legend:
- Areas under Japanese control
- Allies
- Neutral nations
- Allied forces
- Battles
- Atomic bomb

Pearl Harbor
Dec. 1941

Midway
June 1942

PACIFIC OCEAN

Tarawa
Nov. 1943

Guadalcanal
Aug. 1942–Feb. 1943

Coral Sea
May 1942

1,500 mi

1,500 km

750

750

0

0

©2000 maps.com/ MAGELLAN Geographix℠

Saipan, Tinian, & Guam
June–Aug. 1944

Iwo Jima
Feb. 1945

Okinawa
Apr.–June 1945

NEW GUINEA

Port Moresby

AUSTRALIA

Tokyo

JAPAN

Hiroshima
August 6, 1945

Nagasaki
August 9, 1945

MANCHUKUO
(Manchuria)

Vladivostok

Lüshun

Seoul

Pusan

Yellow Sea

MONGOLIA

Peking
Beijing

Shanghai

Yellow R.

Yangtze R.

CHINA

Canton
(Guangzhou)

Hong Kong
(Brit.)

MACAO

South China Sea

FRENCH INDOCHINA

Manila

PHILIPPINES
(US)

Leyte Gulf

N. BORNEO
(Brit.)

BRUNEI
(Brit.)

SARAWAK
(Brit.)

BORNEO

DUTCH EAST INDIES

SUMATRA

Singapore

MALAYA
(Brit.)

Saigon

Bangkok

THAILAND

BURMA

Mandalay

Rangoon

Mekong R.

TIBET

INDIA

Calcutta

Bay of Bengal

INDIAN OCEAN

42°N

15°N

160°E

110°E

42°N

15°N

160°E

110°E

THE BALANCE OF POWER AFTER WORLD WAR II

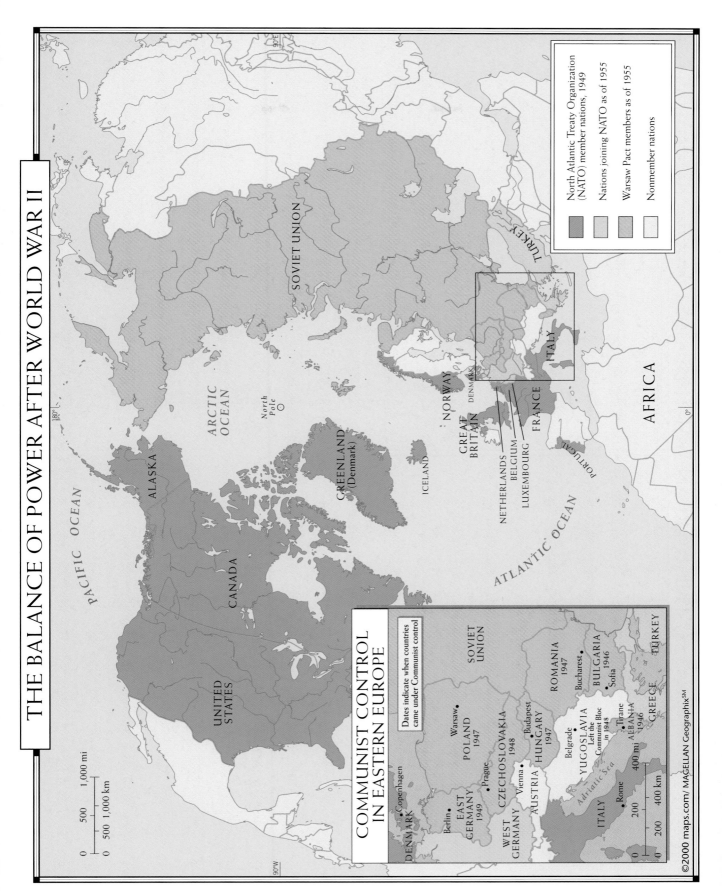

PACIFIC OCEAN

ALASKA

CANADA

UNITED STATES

ARCTIC OCEAN

North Pole

GREENLAND (Denmark)

ICELAND

SOVIET UNION

NORWAY

GREAT BRITAIN

DENMARK

NETHERLANDS
BELGIUM
LUXEMBOURG
FRANCE

PORTUGAL

TURKEY

ITALY

ATLANTIC OCEAN

AFRICA

Legend:
North Atlantic Treaty Organization (NATO) member nations, 1949
Nations joining NATO as of 1955
Warsaw Pact members as of 1955
Nonmember nations

1,000 mi
500   1,000 km
0   500   1,000 km

90°E

180°

90°W

0°

COMMUNIST CONTROL IN EASTERN EUROPE

Dates indicate when countries came under Communist control

DENMARK
Copenhagen

EAST GERMANY 1949
Berlin

WEST GERMANY

POLAND 1947
Warsaw

Prague
CZECHOSLOVAKIA 1948

Vienna
AUSTRIA

Budapest
HUNGARY 1947

ROMANIA 1947
Bucharest

SOVIET UNION

BULGARIA 1946
Sofia

Belgrade
YUGOSLAVIA
Left the Communist Bloc in 1948

Tirane
ALBANIA 1946

Rome
ITALY

Adriatic Sea

GREECE

TURKEY

0   200   400 mi
0   200   400 km

©2000 maps.com/ MAGELLAN Geographix℠

— 43 —

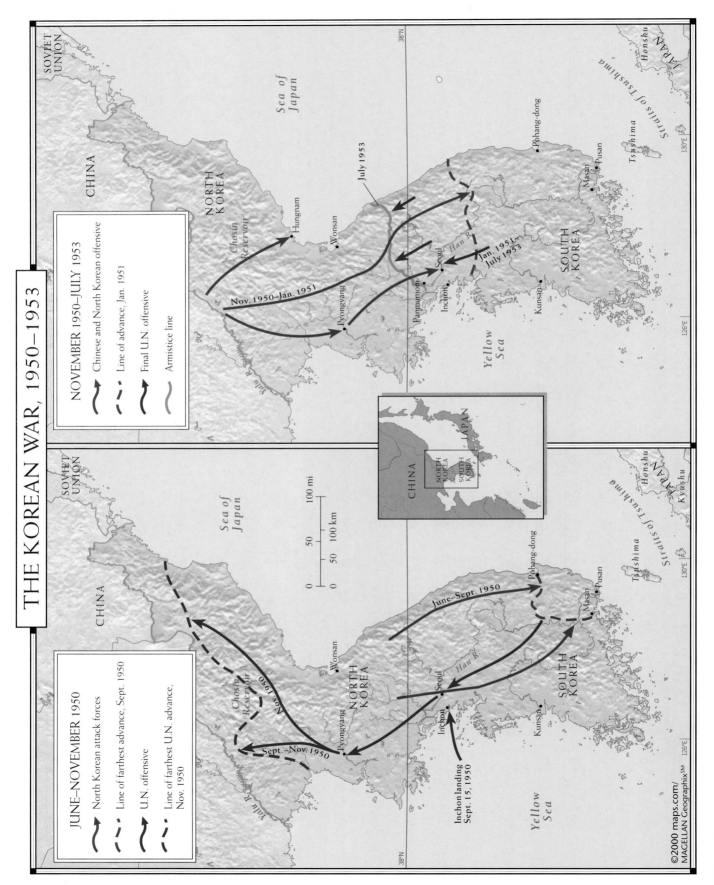

THE KOREAN WAR, 1950–1953

NOVEMBER 1950–JULY 1953

→ Chinese and North Korean offensive

⌐ ⌐ Line of advance, Jan. 1951

→ Final U.N. offensive

∿ Armistice line

Nov. 1950–Jan. 1951

July 1953

Jan. 1951–July 1953

Chosin Reservoir

Hungnam

Wonsan

Pyongyang

Seoul

Panmunjom

Inchon

Kunsan

Pohang-dong

Masan

Pusan

Tsushima

NORTH KOREA

SOUTH KOREA

CHINA

SOVIET UNION

JAPAN

Honshu

Strait of Tsushima

Sea of Japan

Yellow Sea

Han R.

Yalu R.

38°N

126°E

130°E

JUNE–NOVEMBER 1950

→ North Korean attack forces

⌐ ⌐ Line of farthest advance, Sept. 1950

→ U.N. offensive

⌐ ⌐ Line of farthest U.N. advance, Nov. 1950

June–Sept. 1950

Sept.–Nov. 1950

Nov. 1950

Inchon landing Sept. 15, 1950

Chosin Reservoir

Wonsan

Pyongyang

Seoul

Inchon

Kunsan

Pohang-dong

Masan

Pusan

Tsushima

NORTH KOREA

SOUTH KOREA

CHINA

SOVIET UNION

JAPAN

Honshu

Kyushu

Strait of Tsushima

Sea of Japan

Yellow Sea

Han R.

Yalu R.

38°N

126°E

130°E

100 mi

50   100 km

50

0

CHINA

JAPAN

NORTH KOREA

SOUTH KOREA

PUBLIC SCHOOL SEGREGATION BY STATE, 1954

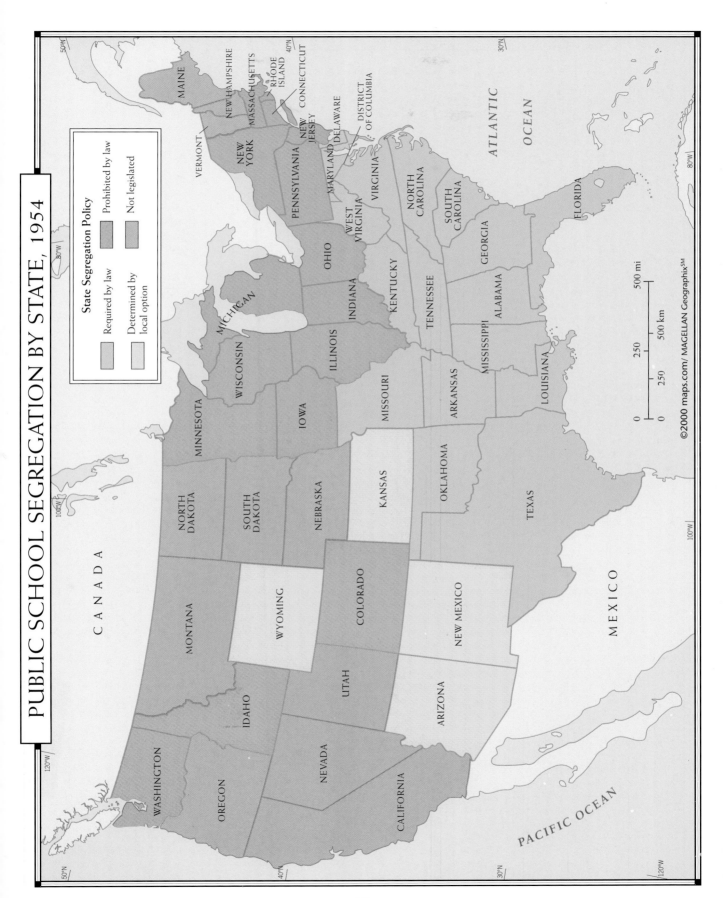

State Segregation Policy

- Required by law
- Prohibited by law
- Determined by local option
- Not legislated

©2000 maps.com/ MAGELLAN Geographix℠

CANADA

MEXICO

ATLANTIC OCEAN

PACIFIC OCEAN

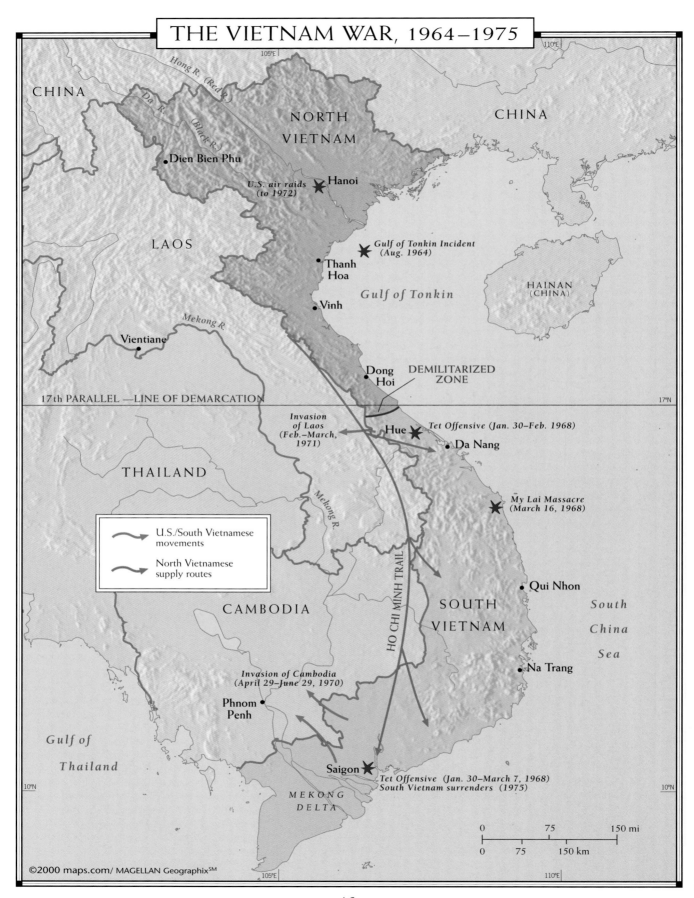

THE VIETNAM WAR, 1964–1975

CHINA

Hong R. (Red R.)

Da R.

Black R.

NORTH VIETNAM

CHINA

• Dien Bien Phu

U.S. air raids (to 1972) ★ Hanoi

LAOS

★ *Gulf of Tonkin Incident (Aug. 1964)*

• Thanh Hoa

HAINAN (CHINA)

Gulf of Tonkin

• Vinh

Mekong R.

Vientiane •

Dong Hoi

DEMILITARIZED ZONE

17th PARALLEL —LINE OF DEMARCATION

17°N

Invasion of Laos (Feb.–March, 1971)

Hue ★ *Tet Offensive (Jan. 30–Feb. 1968)*

• Da Nang

THAILAND

Mekong R.

My Lai Massacre (March 16, 1968) ★

U.S./South Vietnamese movements

North Vietnamese supply routes

• Qui Nhon

CAMBODIA

SOUTH VIETNAM

South China Sea

HO CHI MINH TRAIL

• Na Trang

Invasion of Cambodia (April 29–June 29, 1970)

Phnom Penh •

Gulf of Thailand

Saigon ★ *Tet Offensive (Jan. 30–March 7, 1968)*
South Vietnam surrenders (1975)

MEKONG DELTA

10°N

10°N

| 0 | 75 | 150 mi |

| 0 | 75 | 150 km |

©2000 maps.com/ MAGELLAN Geographix℠

105°E

110°E

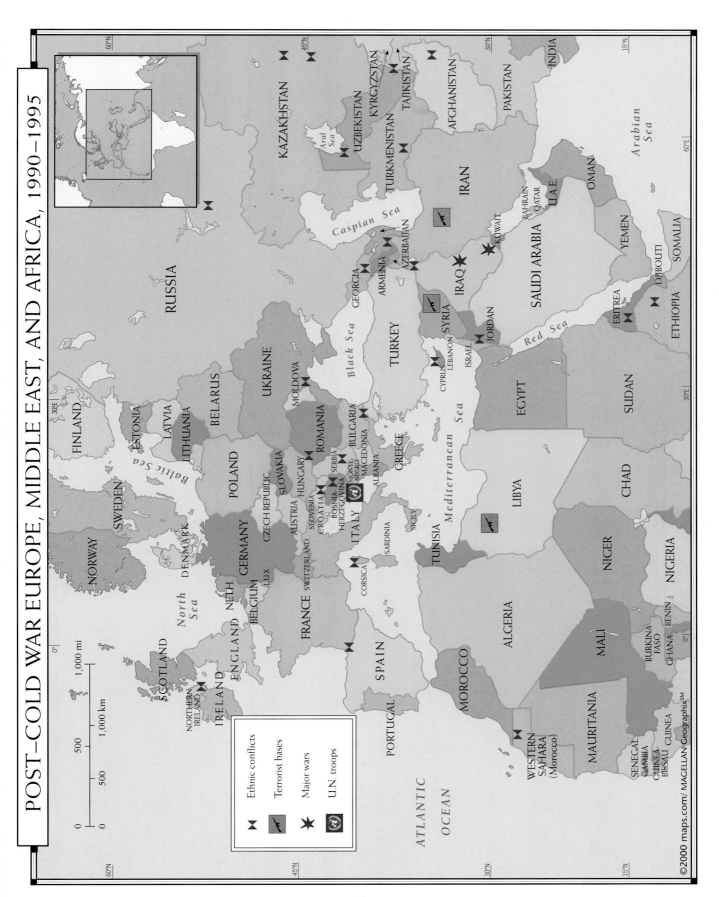

POST–COLD WAR EUROPE, MIDDLE EAST, AND AFRICA, 1990–1995

Legend:
- Ethnic conflicts
- Terrorist bases
- Major wars
- U.N. troops

©2000 maps.com/ MAGELLAN Geographix℠

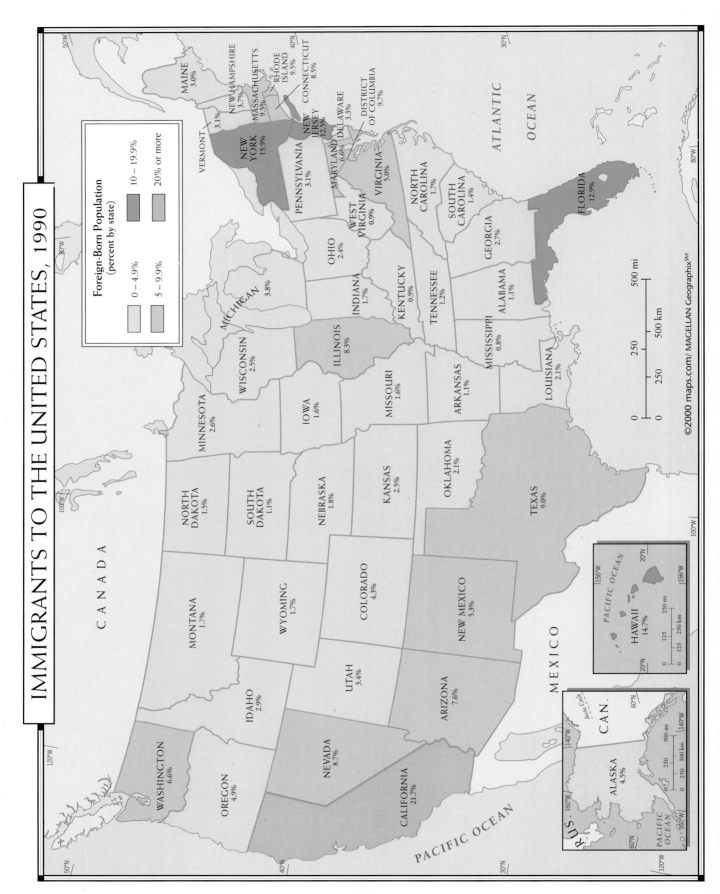

IMMIGRANTS TO THE UNITED STATES, 1990

Foreign-Born Population
(percent by state)

- 0 – 4.9%
- 5 – 9.9%
- 10 – 19.9%
- 20% or more

MAINE 3.0%
NEW HAMPSHIRE 3.7%
VERMONT 3.1%
MASSACHUSETTS 9.5%
RHODE ISLAND 9.5%
CONNECTICUT 8.5%
NEW YORK 15.9%
NEW JERSEY 12.5%
DELAWARE 3.3%
DISTRICT OF COLUMBIA 9.7%
PENNSYLVANIA 3.1%
MARYLAND 6.6%
VIRGINIA 5.0%
WEST VIRGINIA 0.9%
NORTH CAROLINA 1.7%
SOUTH CAROLINA 1.4%
OHIO 2.4%
KENTUCKY 0.9%
TENNESSEE 1.2%
GEORGIA 2.7%
ALABAMA 1.1%
FLORIDA 12.9%
MICHIGAN 3.8%
INDIANA 1.7%
ILLINOIS 8.3%
WISCONSIN 2.5%
IOWA 1.6%
MISSOURI 1.6%
ARKANSAS 1.1%
MISSISSIPPI 0.8%
LOUISIANA 2.1%
MINNESOTA 2.6%
NORTH DAKOTA 1.5%
SOUTH DAKOTA 1.1%
NEBRASKA 1.8%
KANSAS 2.5%
OKLAHOMA 2.1%
TEXAS 9.0%
MONTANA 1.7%
WYOMING 1.7%
COLORADO 4.3%
NEW MEXICO 5.3%
IDAHO 2.9%
UTAH 3.4%
ARIZONA 7.6%
NEVADA 8.7%
CALIFORNIA 21.7%
WASHINGTON 6.6%
OREGON 4.9%

HAWAII 14.7%
ALASKA 4.5%

ATLANTIC OCEAN
PACIFIC OCEAN
CANADA
MEXICO
PACIFIC OCEAN

©2000 maps.com/ MAGELLAN Geographix℠

500 mi
500 km
250
250
0
0

– 48 –